What GOD WANTS to Do FOR YOU

JIM GEORGE

HARVEST HOUSE PUBLISHERS

EUGENE, OREGON

WHAT GOD WANTS TO DO FOR YOU
Originally titled *Powerful Promises for Every Couple*
Copyright © 2004 by Jim George
Published by Harvest House Publishers
Eugene, Oregon 97402

ISBN-13: 978-0-7369-1783-4
ISBN-10: 0-7369-1783-7

Printed in the United States of America

06 07 08 09 10 11 12 13 / BP-MS / 10 9 8 7 6 5 4 3 2 1

Contents

A Word of Welcome   7

God's Powerful Promises...to You   11

1. God's Powerful Promise of...Answered Prayer . . .   17

2. God's Powerful Promise of...Change   25

3. God's Powerful Promise of...Comfort.   33

4. God's Powerful Promise of...Completion   41

5. God's Powerful Promise of...Courage   49

6. God's Powerful Promise of...Deliverance   57

7. God's Powerful Promise of...Forgiveness   65

8. God's Powerful Promise of...Grace   73

9. God's Powerful Promise of...Guidance.   81

10. God's Powerful Promise of...Hope.   89

11. God's Powerful Promise of...Life   97

12. God's Powerful Promise of...Love 105

13. God's Powerful Promise of...Peace 113

14. God's Powerful Promise of...Power 121

15. God's Powerful Promise of...Presence 129

16. God's Powerful Promise of...Provision. 137

17. God's Powerful Promise of...Purpose. 145

18. God's Powerful Promise of...Rest. 153

19. God's Powerful Promise of...Self-Discipline 161

20. God's Powerful Promise of...Strength. 171

21. God's Powerful Promise of...Success 179

22. God's Powerful Promise of...Victory 189

23. God's Powerful Promise of...Wisdom. 199

24. God's Powerful Promise of...Worth 209

God's Promises...and Your Character 215

Study Guide 219

Notes 297

A Word of Welcome

Recently I was sitting on the couch, skimming through a book dealing with the difficulties and issues of life. The categories of problems and topics covered a vast range—

> from anxiety to temptation
> from pride to money matters
> from overcoming failure to dealing with loss
> from fighting fear to searching for purpose
> from being truthful to trusting God
> from handling pain to falling in love
> from starting over to facing death

As I read along, I was thinking, *Yes!* and, *Been there, done that!* Ten pages later, I looked up and laughed, feeling, *Boy, oh boy, is that ever me!*

Are you with me? Do any of the above plights relate to your life? And can you add to the list?

Of course you can! You're human. And, like me, you probably wonder, *Where can I go for help with difficult issues? Is there hope? How can I handle these challenges?*

Now comes the good news. There is help...and hope! That help comes to you from God. God wants to make His powerful promises available to aid you in handling your roles and responsibilities, and in improving your life.

So come on! Join me in a treasure hunt, in the adventure of discovering what God wants to do for you as we look at just a handful of the thousands of promises that God gives to every one of His children. Whether you are one day old in the Lord or you've been walking with God for decades, these powerful promises are yours.

And if you'd like to receive an even greater blessing, you can discover more about God's promises by taking a little extra time to work through the Study Guide section at the back of the book. You will be pleasantly surprised to find your heart miraculously transformed by God's Word. The practical insights and helpful hints in these study questions will motivate and enable you to put God's powerful promises to work in every area of your life.

And I encourage you to share these promises with others. Share your book with your spouse, or a friend. Share it in a men's study, or a ladies' group, or your couples class. And don't forget to share it with your children whatever their ages!

And I purpose to pray for you. I want you to know God's promises. And I want you to experience God's peace and power as you face each day and each challenge armed with an arsenal of God's promises for you.

By His grace,

Jim George

Every Divine promise
is built upon four pillars:
God's holiness,
    which will not suffer Him to deceive;
His goodness,
    which will not suffer Him to forget;
His truth,
    which will not suffer Him to change; and
His power,
    which makes Him able to accomplish![1]

God's Powerful Promises
to You

*There has not failed one word
of all His good promise.*
1 KINGS 8:56 (NKJV)

Greetings...and welcome to this exciting, encouraging, and helpful book! How can I make such a claim? Because this is a book about discovering and applying the wisdom and power God promises to us for managing the challenges we face every day.

As we launch our exploration of what God wants to do for us, let's take a few minutes to gain a better understanding of God's promises.

The Nature of a Promise

What is a promise? The dictionary defines the word *promise* as "a statement, either oral or written, assuring that one will or will not do something." It's a vow or a pledge.

You've probably made a few vows and pledges in your lifetime—to your spouse when you exchanged wedding vows and pledged your undying love, to your local church as a member, to a company's code of ethics, to a branch of the government, to the armed forces, even to a close friend. So you have some experience with promises, vows, and pledges.

The Nature of God

In this book we are looking at the promises of God...and God's power to follow through and keep His promises. This is important because *the power of a promise depends on the one making the promise.*

And, dear reading friend, that means you can trust in God's promises. Why? Because of God's nature and character. God is described as the "God, who cannot lie" (Titus 1:2). Therefore, you can be confident that if there is a promise in God's Word that has an application for you, you can accept that promise with full assurance. God will do His part to fulfill that promise. It's His nature. And God cannot lie!

Revisit the quote at the beginning of this prologue on God's powerful promises, and realize again that the power of God's *promises* rests in the power of God *Himself!*

The Nature of Promises in the Bible

Here's something else to keep in mind as you read: *Many of*

God's promises are limited to specific people or groups of people, but many are unlimited and apply to our lives as well.

For example, the verse at the beginning of this chapter, while given to a *specific group of people*, has application today for *you and me as well*. Here's the story behind the promise...

King Solomon, David's son, had just offered up a prayer of dedication to God for the newly completed temple in Jerusalem. In that prayer, Solomon recounted before the Lord all that God had done concerning His people. After completing his prayer, Solomon turned around and made this statement: "Blessed be the LORD, who has given rest to His people Israel, according to all that He promised; not one word has failed of all His good promise" (1 Kings 8:56).

Solomon reminded the people of Israel that God always keeps His promises. And this is also a good reminder to us. God always kept His promises to Israel, and God, in His consistency, will always keep His promises to us.

The Nature of God's Promises to You

Finally, realize that *many of God's promises are conditional*. That means God will do something or give something; but, in return, we are to do something or give something as well. Take this promise to the nation of Israel as an example:

> Now it shall be, if you will diligently obey the LORD your God, being careful to do all His commandments which I command you today, the LORD your God will set you high above all the nations of the earth (Deuteronomy 28:1).

That's a great promise, isn't it? God promised to make His people greater than any other nation on earth. But note who the promise was given to and the condition: *The people of Israel* had to "obey the Lord."

As You Begin...

When working your way through this book, be sure to keep these facts in mind:

—⁓— God is able to fulfill His promises.

—⁓— God always keeps His promises.

—⁓— God made some promises to specific people.

—⁓— God made some promises conditional.

—⁓— God made some promises unconditional.

To receive the power and blessing of God attached to His precious and magnificent promises (2 Peter 1:4), you will be expected to do your part (by His grace!). But please remember that what is asked of you will not be burdensome. In fact, God promises to provide the resources for you to do your part. What a deal!

Putting God's Power to Work

Now, here comes the fun! Each chapter in *What God Wants to Do for You* will end with an application section like this one. This will be your opportunity to embrace and respond to the particular promise spotlighted under the microscope. So here we go! As you begin...

✓ *Are you willing...* to put God's promises to work in your life? The Bible offers many powerful promises (some estimates say 30,000-plus![2]). God's promises are there for the taking. God would not offer what He is unable or unwilling to give. So you can be assured of the legitimacy of His promises. When it comes to putting God's powerful promises to work in your life, the issue will never be with God. No, it will always be with you and your willingness to do your part to put God's power and promises to work. Are you willing?

✓ *Are you willing...* to do what God asks of you? I pray that you are, because tapping into the power of God's promises will demand something from and of you. "What will be required of me?" you ask. In a word, *obedience.*

And before you throw your hands up in defeat, realize that God is not asking for perfection. No, God knows us well, and He knows our weaknesses. He is only asking for progression—progression indicated by...

—a willingness to follow God even though at times you stumble and fall (Philippians 3:14),

—a willingness to ask for forgiveness when you falter (1 John 1:9), and

—a willingness to stay in the battle (and it is a battle!) of becoming a man or a woman after God's own heart (Acts 13:22).

The truth is, the promises are yours. Are you ready and willing to put them to work in your life? If so, read on to discover what God wants to do for you!

*Prayer is a powerful thing,
for God has bound and tied Himself thereto.
None can believe how powerful prayer is,
and what it is able to effect,
but those who have learned it by experience.*

—MARTIN LUTHER

1

God's Powerful Promise of
Answered Prayer

W here do you live? My wife, Elizabeth, and I happen to live in a house that sits on a hill. That means our home was built with several levels. Each day one of us writes on one level in the house and the other writes on another. To communicate with each other from office to office while we're working on our manuscripts, we use walkie-talkies.

One day recently when our grandchildren were with us, they spotted the walkie-talkies and, of course, they wanted to talk on them. After explaining how they worked, we gave one to Jacob and one to Katie, who at the time of this writing are five and four years old respectively.

Well, it wasn't long before both children came back, pagers in hand, crying and complaining that the walkie-talkies were broken. Because they were too young to understand how to send and receive messages, Jacob and Katie were sure the problem was with the walkie-talkies.

Discovering the Promise

Friend, we are probably all a lot like our grandchildren: We don't understand how to communicate with God! Then, when we think our prayers aren't being answered, we tend to get discouraged and blame God. We think God is the problem. We question, "Why isn't God answering my prayers?" But as we look at God's promise of answered prayer, you will see that God always comes through. Hear Jesus Himself offer this promise:

> *Ask, and it shall be given to you;*
> *seek, and you shall find;*
> *knock, and it shall be opened to you.*
> *For everyone who asks receives,*
> *and he who seeks finds,*
> *and to him who knocks it shall be opened.*
> MATTHEW 7:7-8

God does answer our prayers! In fact, He promises to answer us when we pray. And sometimes He answers when we don't even know how to pray about a certain issue. When that happens, the Holy Spirit steps in and "intercedes for us" (Romans 8:26). But usually we know what our needs are, and who or what we should be praying for. So God asks us to *ask*.

As we move ahead in our understanding of God's powerful promise of answered prayer, keep in mind that to enjoy the promise, our requests must be...

—in faith (Matthew 21:22),

—without selfish motives (James 4:3), and

—according to the will of God (1 John 5:14-15).

Understanding the Promise

As we pause and think about prayer, praying, and answered prayer, two long-standing issues surface:

1. *Why do we have such a hard time with prayer?*

The answer to this question may lie in the fact that many people seem to have difficulty asking...asking for directions, asking for help of any kind, and specifically, asking for help from God by praying! We simply never get around to asking; therefore, we're never aware of any answers.

2. *Why don't we pray more often?*

Well, we've hit the jackpot on this one! Here are at least nine reasons why we don't pray more often. Feel free to add to the list as you read on.

Worldliness—We live in the world, but are not of the world (John 17:16). There is no voice in the world admonishing us to pray. Prayer is a spiritual exercise. Therefore, we must take the initiative to be spiritually minded. We must ask for spiritual assistance and blessings.

Busyness—We are so busy we think we are too busy to take time to stop and ask anything of God. Yet we are never too busy to play golf, go shopping, or attend our child's soccer game. We're never too busy to do what is important or meaningful to us. So where is prayer on your busy schedule? For many Christians, it's nowhere!

Faithlessness—For whatever reason, we doubt that things might have a different outcome due to faithful and earnest prayer on our part. But if we had confidence and believed that God answers prayer, we would not be able to wait to come into His presence with our needs and requests! We'd be asking...and we'd be enjoying...God's answers! Perhaps James's assessment is true in your failure to enjoy answers to your prayers—"You do not have because *you do not ask*" (James 4:2).

Distance—We feel distant from God because we fail to talk to Him, so we feel like strangers around Him. God hasn't changed, moved, disappeared, or lost interest in you. Close the gap—take a simple step and talk to God. The more you talk, the more you'll communicate. And the more you communicate, the more opportunities you'll have to ask. And the more you ask, the more answers you'll receive.

Ignorance—We don't understand God's power and goodness. We don't grasp His desire and His ability to provide "exceeding abundantly beyond all that we ask or think" (Ephesians 3:20) and to "supply all of [our] needs" (Philippians 4:19). If we did, we would pray.

Sinfulness—We allow sin to build a barrier between us and a caring God. What did the psalmist say? "If I regard iniquity in my heart, the Lord will not hear" (Psalm 66:18 NKJV). But when we confess our sin, the Lord's ears are open to our cries (Psalm

34:15), and the odds of having our prayers answered go sky high!

Pridefulness—We, in essence, say to God, "I don't need You, God. I can take care of this myself." Think about this: "The self-sufficient do not pray, the self-satisfied will not pray, the self-righteous cannot pray."[3]

Inexperience—We don't pray; therefore, we don't know how to pray...so we don't pray! Prayer is like any skill—it becomes easier with repetition. The more we pray, the more we know how to pray. And the more we pray, the more answers to prayer we experience.

Laziness—Maybe this is the saddest excuse of all. We are just not willing to make the effort to pray, no matter how important it is...which, of course, affects our chances of having our prayers answered. *Lord, may we never get to this place in our spiritual life!*

Putting God's Power to Work

Now, how can you experience answers to your prayers and concerns? And how can you experience the joy of God's power in your life? How can you begin to develop a better prayer life? How can you realize and revel in God's powerful promise to answer your prayers?

✓ *Take an honest look*...at the excuses you are using for not praying. You can begin with the nine reasons we fail to pray. Identify the one that is most obvious in your life. Then ask God to help you overcome this excuse so that you can become a better pray-er. Imagine how sweet the answers to your prayers will taste when you conquer this one hurdle.

✓ *Start a prayer list or notebook....*Use a section in your daily planner or appointment book as the beginning of a list of people and things to pray for. Like any businessperson, be organized as you do business with God. Then, like an accountant, be prepared to record the answers as they come!

✓ *Memorize one of God's promises...*of answered prayer. Start with the promise highlighted in this chapter. It may help to remember the abbreviated version of this promise...A-S-K:

A sk...and you will receive

S eek...and you will find

K nock...and it will be opened

✓ *Talk to God...*throughout your day—in the car, in the shower, while jogging or running errands. Get better acquainted with God.

✓ *Set an initial goal...*of praying five minutes a day, or five minutes longer, if you're already praying regularly. It stands to reason that the more time you spend in prayer, the more time you have to "let your requests be made known to God" (Philippians 4:6)...and the more answers to your prayers you will receive.

Someone once said,
"I am not afraid to grow old.
I'm afraid I'll grow old and be the
same as I am now."
Christianity would be a pointless journey
if we failed to show any improvement
in our walk with our Lord,
in our love for others,
in our knowledge of God.
—Source unknown

2

God's Powerful Promise of
Change

I'm a former member of the medical field, which means I still read medical journals and clip the articles that catch my eye. One such article was a report on a study that was conducted on several thousand men and women who had lived beyond their life expectancy. Many of the people in the study were well into their nineties, and some were more than 100 years old. In assessing the secrets to longevity, the researchers looked at personality, dietary habits, physical exercise, and the abuse of substances such as alcohol and tobacco.

While reading along, I immediately assumed that the longevity factor had to be attributed to what these people ate or drank. I surmised, "They must have eaten tofu and seaweed and drank gallons of purified water from some guarded mountain stream!"

But, surprise of surprises, the researchers reported that the common denominator was not what these people did or did not consume. No, most of these very, very senior citizens had placed few restrictions on their physical habits.

Do you know what the common thread was that ran through the lives of all these "survivors"? In one word, it was *adapt-ability*. These people apparently lived longer because they had an ability to change—change with the seasons of their lives, change with the deaths of spouses, change with their surround-ings. Needless to say, that article gave me greater insight into the importance of our ability to adapt to change.

Discovering the Promise

How do you rate in the Change Department? Change is like the weather in my home state of Oklahoma. "Okies" have a saying: "If you don't like the weather now, wait a few minutes!" Change, like Oklahoma weather, is inevitable and unpredict-able. Like it or not, we are all part of a changing world. Jobs come and go. The size of the family keeps expanding...and contracting. Relationships and health are uncertain. Life has its changing seasons. And with each one, you must adapt.

But in spite of the constancy of change and our need to adapt to it in one way or another, everyone has an aversion to change—especially when things seem to be going well. "Why do I need to change?" you ask. "I'm doing great! Things are fine at home. I have my health. I have job security" (...or so you think!).

Then one day you wake up to find that you have become obsolete in the marketplace, and your reason for being with your company no longer exists. Or, a conflict arises between you and your spouse, which exposes some cracks in your marriage. In many cases, such scenarios occur because someone didn't grow professionally or maritally, and didn't adapt to meet life's changes.

Change is not limited to the physical, marital, and vocational realms. In fact, change is more critical in the spiritual realm than in all the others. Why? Because we serve a God whose specialty is change and transformation.

Ever since the fall of Adam and Eve in the Garden of Eden, God has desired to call the lost back to Him and create a race of spiritually redeemed people—a people who would love Him, follow Him, and obey Him. God's plan for bringing this about came to a climax with the incarnation of Jesus Christ. It's because of Christ's life, death, and resurrection that salvation is possible. When we come into a relationship with Christ, God promises—*promises*—to bring about a radical change in our lives! How radical? God is committed to nothing less than an entirely new order of creation. This is how His powerful promise reads:

> *If any man is in Christ, he is a new creature;*
> *the old things passed away;*
> *behold, new things have come.*
> 2 CORINTHIANS 5:17

Understanding the Promise

Dear friend, God is not interested in preserving the status quo. In the Old Testament, He promised to give His people "a new heart" and put "a new spirit" in them, to take away their "heart of stone" and replace it with "a heart of flesh" (Ezekiel 36:26). And as we look at New Testament scripture, we see that in this new spiritual order, change is the essential element. What does this change-process look like?

1. *The starting point for change is spiritual transformation.*

God's promise of change states that when we are *in Christ*, we become *new creatures*. God gives us "a new heart." We are not re-formed, re-habilitated, or re-programmed. Instead we are re-created—we experience the "new birth" (John 3:3). We now live in vital union with Christ (Colossians 2:6), under a new Master, which brings about further change.

What good news! When you are *in Christ,* everything changes! Outward conditions and circumstances may be the same, but they shine with a new beauty and life. Which means...

2. *Inward change shows itself outwardly.*

"You can tell the tree by the fruit" is an old saying that actually has biblical roots (see Matthew 7:17-20). The same is true of your life and the "fruit" it produces. If you are transformed inwardly, then that change leads to some pretty drastic outward change—*old things passed away!* Your worldly desires from your old life either vanish instantly or fade away. Amazingly, you begin to desire the things of God. Now, *that's* change!

These new inward desires for God constantly work themselves in, out, and through your life to bring about change, to conform you into the "image" of your Savior, Jesus Christ (2 Corinthians 3:18). When you have Christ in you, He shines forth from your life. Imagine the difference that makes in a life!

3. *Change does not always happen quickly.*

Some old desires drop away quickly. These are usually sinful *actions*. A person stops lying, cleans up his or her language, puts away harmful habits. And behold, in their place, *new things have come!* They are part of the constant process of change that is taking place and will continue on in the future.

But some of the old ways are hard to eradicate. They are the lingering old *attitudes* that are not so quickly changed—attitudes such as anger, greed, pride, selfishness, ambition, lust, jealousy, to name just a few.

Dear reader, thank God for the quick changes in your outward actions. But be on guard against growing impatient and feeling like giving up because change seems to be going much slower in the area of mastering your old attitudes. That's when you must remember that your journey to a complete spiritual makeover is a lifelong process. Changes and victories will come, but some old habits and attitudes die hard. So please be patient...and be patient with others!

Again, thank God for the progress you have already made. Then ask Him for strength to continue the process. Because...

4. *Change is a constant process.*

Change can be either good or bad. When change occurs, you are either growing in faith and knowledge...or you are slipping back into old ways, old habits, old actions, and old attitudes. You simply cannot rest on past change! *Today* is a new day with new challenges for you. You must ask God *today* for His enabling power to further conform you into the image of His Son.

Then *tomorrow* you must get up (again) and ask God (again) for power (again) for one more day of change. Do whatever you must to ensure that the old ways don't creep back into your life and cause you to slip into your former sinful patterns. The battle for godly change is constant. And, let's face it, it will be ongoing until we meet our Savior face to face.

Putting God's Power to Work

How wonderful it is to realize that as a Christian man or woman, you are a brand-new person—*a new creature*—in Jesus Christ. The slate is clean. The Holy Spirit has invaded your heart, soul, and body with new life, and nothing is the same. So what are you going to do about this inward change, this miraculous transformation?

Ask yourself the questions that follow. They will help you do your part in God's plan so that you can be a mirror "that brightly reflects the glory of the Lord. And as the Spirit of the Lord works within you, you become more and more like him and reflect his glory even more" (2 Corinthians 3:18 NLT).

- ✓ *Ask*—How has my life changed since accepting Christ? Jot down three positive major changes that have occurred since you became a new creation (2 Corinthians 5:17). Then thank God for these.

- ✓ *Ask*—What further changes does God want me to make in my life that will better reflect that I am His child? List at least two. Then ask God for His help in making those changes.

- ✓ *Ask*—your spouse, a trusted friend, or mentor to share any positive changes observed in your conduct and character. Then, if you are really courageous, ask if there are any further areas of needed change. Express your thanks to this trusted person...and then ask God for His help.

What a gracious God we have!
Able to count the myriads of stars
studding the sky,
He condescends to heal "the brokenhearted"
and to bind up "their wounds."
With His majesty there is mercy.
Sovereign though He is,
He is ever the sympathizer![4]

3

God's Powerful Promise of
Comfort

When you first picked up this book about God's promises to you, you probably looked first at the table of contents. Your eyes immediately spotted a number of very desirable and promised traits such as strength, power, wisdom, courage, and victory. That's because these assurances have great appeal to your everyday needs in your life, your marriage, and your work. The promises of valiant qualities such as these provide the kind of motivation a soldier would cling to during battle. And, whether you realize it or not, you are a soldier—a soldier for Jesus Christ. And the promises of these kinds of qualities are very fitting for you as you go to war on your various daily battlefronts at home, at work, or in other places.

But tucked in the midst of the powerful promises featured in this book is a promise from God that has a softer, more tender feel to it. When people think of comfort, they usually think immediately of a woman. A woman lovingly nurtures her husband, her children, her friends, you name it—it's her nature! And through all of the times of heartache and pain, she is right there to offer comfort to all.

Discovering the Promise

Are we correct to attribute comfort only to the female side of the human species? Is a woman the only one to have and show compassion and offer comfort? Is a guy's manhood reluctant to the idea that he, too, should have a compassionate side?

Well, if you desire to become more "Godlike" and "Christlike" in your actions and attitudes, then look at this next assurance from God. In it, we discover a powerful promise that is intimate, tender, and heartwarming. It is a picture of God, the Father, consoling His own.

> *Blessed be the God and Father*
> *of our Lord Jesus Christ,*
> *the Father of mercies and God of all comfort;*
> *who comforts us in all our affliction.*
> 2 CORINTHIANS 1:3-4

Understanding the Promise

To many Christians, this promise is the most compelling passage on comfort found in the New Testament. The apostle Paul speaks repeatedly about the concept of comfort (2 Corinthians 1:1-7). And he speaks specifically of God's promise of comfort for those of His children who are experiencing suffering and hardship.

1. *God's comfort is a part of His nature.*

To the casual observer of biblical truth, it might seem that God is a vengeful, angry deity who takes pleasure in inflicting pain on His creation. But as we examine this promise of God's comfort, we see the exact opposite—that God is referred to as "the Father of mercies." It's a part of His nature. Scripture describes God as a father who has "compassion" for His children and whose "lovingkindness...is from everlasting to everlasting" (Psalm 103:13,17). So we can see that compassion is a constant and significant part of God's nature. Compassion is God's love that extends itself to sinners and to His hurting children and cares for them and transforms them.

2. *God's comfort is our enabler.*

Here's a fact to hang on to in your times of suffering: The more you suffer, the more comfort God gives you. Paul put it this way: God "comforts us in all our affliction," giving us His strength, encouragement, and hope to endure our trials. This is a powerful promise you can count on in *all* your affliction!

Paul also adds that God is "the God of all comfort." He is always ready to comfort you. Whatever your hardship—big or small—it doesn't matter, for the God of *all* comfort is available to help you. Are you hurting physically or emotionally? Are things not going well at work? At home? Is there some temptation you are struggling with, or an area in which you need support? Do you need encouragement? In all of these and more, believe it—God is there to help and to comfort! The all-powerful God who transcends all also chooses to "reach down" and heal the brokenhearted and bind up their wounds (Psalm 147:3). His enablement is a promise!

3. *God's comfort is our teacher.*

There's an added bonus to your painful experiences: Your suffering and God's comfort become your teacher so that the more you suffer and the more comfort God gives you, then the more comfort you have to pass on to those who are suffering...beginning right at home!

Friend, this was Paul's point when he wrote about the reciprocal nature of comfort: God "comforts us in all our affliction *so that* we may be able to comfort those who are in any affliction with the comfort with which we ourselves are comforted by God" (2 Corinthians 1:4).

So what are we to do with the comfort God gives us? Enjoy it, to be sure! Let it teach us, most definitely! But be faithful to pass it on to others who are suffering, beginning at home. Every trial you and I endure, through God's grace, helps us comfort others when they are suffering hardships. God's blessed comfort is not only to cheer *us* up, but it is also intended to cheer *others* too.

Putting God's Power to Work

God is truly the God of all comfort. He ministers to the hurting and to the brokenhearted in at least two ways: through His Spirit, and through His words of comfort in the Bible. But at other times God uses *you,* to administer comfort.

Now, we all know it's not easy to be strong in the Comfort Department! But we need to accept the fact that at times God wants to use us as instruments of comfort in someone else's life—perhaps a spouse, a family member, a close friend or neighbor, someone at church, or even a fellow worker.

Whoever God brings across your path to comfort, take it as a compliment. Learn to share the comfort you've received from God. Don't shy away from this important ministry to others. Instead...

✓ *Develop*...a heart of compassion (Colossians 3:12). Jesus is our perfect example. He constantly demonstrated compassion as He walked this earth, comforting any and all. Make the Master your model.

✓ *Look*...for opportunities to show compassion and comfort. And again, begin at home! Sometimes you comfort a person in pain by just being with him or her. Maybe all it takes is a pat on the shoulder, a hug, or just being available if and when the other person wants to talk. Words are not the only way to comfort.

✓ *Don't*...lecture or sermonize. Remember, the other person is in pain, distraught, or grieving. Now may not be the best time to tell him or her how to respond or act while going through a difficult situation.

✓ *Don't*...accuse or criticize. Now is probably not the best time to tell someone what he or she should or should not have done. There will be other times for that person to hear from you and others. For now, just be there for the one who is in pain.

✓ *Think*...back on a time when you were hurting and how it felt. Then empathize by remembering what God did to encourage you. Use your past experiences to let the one who is suffering know that you have faced pain, too.

Share how you were encouraged, and how you eventually were able to overcome the hurt or discouragement. The voice of Matthew Henry rises up from the past to remind us that "we speak best of God and His goodness when we speak from our own experience."[5]

✓   *Read*...this list often when *you* need to be comforted:

Difficulties can...

deepen your faith,
teach patience,
develop maturity,
build wisdom,
force you to pray, and
remind you of what is truly important.

Tough times demand...

a strong mind,
a great heart,
a true faith, and
ready hands.[6]

Now to Him
who is able to keep you from stumbling,
and to make you stand in the presence of His glory
blameless with great joy,
to the only God our Savior,
through Jesus Christ our Lord,
be glory, majesty, dominion and authority,
before all time and now and forever.
Amen.
—JUDE 24-25

4

God's Powerful Promise of
Completion

Are you a person who loves to start projects, practices, and ministries? I have fit this description for years. And it's been a great joy to see many of my ventures come to pass and continue on.

But here's a confession—I can also tend to not finish some of my projects (and I have a storage unit to prove it!). Beginning a new undertaking is thrilling, especially when you're a visionary and have lots of ideas. But, oh boy, as I begin to carry out that venture, is it ever easy to get distracted by yet another new dream...and then, before I know it, I'm off and running with that latest inspiration!

That's when I realize how fortunate I am to have other dear souls who come alongside me to help finish what I've started. On the top of my "thanksgiving" list to God are the names of many wonderful friends and committed finishers. But most of all, I—and you—can thank God that when it comes to our eternal destiny, *He* is both a starter *and* a finisher!

Discovering the Promise

Do you ever feel that you are not making much progress in your spiritual life? That you take two steps forward in your growth...only to fall back one (or is it two?)? Are you becoming discouraged by shortcomings and slow growth? Do you feel unfinished? Incomplete?

Well, take heart, my friend. When God starts a project (that's you!), He completes it. God has promised that He will help each of us who embraces His Son as Savior to grow in His grace until He has completed—yes, *completed!*—His work in our lives.

That's what this present promise is all about. When the apostle Paul wrote his letter to the believers in the Philippian church, he expressed excitement because he had heard that his beloved friends were maturing in their Christian faith. And as he wrote to his comrades-in-Christ, Paul shared his confidence that God would be faithful to continue the spiritual growth process in their lives.

And friend, God will continue that process until it is completed in you as well. That's a promise! Read it for yourself. Read Paul's powerful, encouraging, and comforting words of confidence to his friends...and to you!

For I am confident of this very thing,
that He who began a good work in you
will perfect it until the day of Christ Jesus.
PHILIPPIANS 1:6

Understanding the Promise

Think about it: Your physical life started with your birth. The same is true regarding your spiritual life. It too started with a birth—the "new birth" of salvation (John 3:7)—and will continue on until you see your Lord face to face (1 John 3:2). In sharing this promise of completion, Paul wanted to reassure his readers, and us today as well, that no matter what might happen along the way, God's work cannot be stopped. His work in our lives will continue until completion.

Why was Paul so confident about this? Because he knew how God works in a believer's life. Here's "God's Plan for Spiritual Growth."

1. *God's work in our salvation.*

God's work in our lives started in eternity when a sovereign God determined, by His grace, to redeem us to Himself (2 Timothy 1:9). God's work continued on as He sent His Son, the sinless Lord Jesus Christ, to die for sinners...for you and for me. Then, at the point in time when we trusted in Christ, salvation took root, and God *began a good work* in us.

Did you notice my use of the word *sovereign?* This term describes a king or ruler who has complete power. And isn't that an accurate description of our God? Nothing, and no one, has more power than God. He has all the power needed to run His universe. Nothing has happened, can happen, or will happen without God's knowledge. So when Paul says, "He who

began a good work in you will perfect it," we can be confident
that God is powerful enough to complete the work He began
at salvation.

The completion process has begun—
that's salvation.

2. *God's work in us.*

God's work in our lives didn't stop at salvation. No, our great
God has given us His Holy Spirit to work *in* us. Jesus said, "I
will ask the Father, and He will give you another Helper, that He
may be with you forever, that is the Spirit of truth....He abides
with you, and will be in you" (John 14:16-17).

Can you imagine? God is living in you! Friend, God is going
to ensure that you grow more like His Son, that you grow more
Christlike. He has given you a resident tutor to enable you to be
more like Jesus every day and to guide you into all truth (John
16:13). Now, that should revolutionize any life!

The completion process continues—
that's sanctification.

3. *God's work for us.*

As we've already noted, it's hard for us to be finishers. But thank
the Lord that He is a finisher! God is the author and finisher of
our faith (Hebrews 12:2). Jesus Christ saved us, and now He lives
to pray for us and plead for us (Hebrews 7:25). And aren't you so
very grateful? His faithfulness will carry us *until the day of Jesus*
Christ, until we meet Him face-to-face. That's the finish line!

How big is your God? The Bible says your God is in control
of all things—and that includes your future (and the path your
life has taken, is taking, and will take). God will ensure that you

cross the finish line, complete and perfect in Him. Therefore, you can live your life without any doubts or fears. Nothing and no one can stop God's good work in you (Romans 8:28-29).

Why not pause for a moment and marvel at God's goodness? And then offer up a prayer of gratitude for God's powerful promise of completion.

> *The completion process will be finished—*
> *that's glorification.*

Putting God's Power to Work

Isn't it great to know, and then to believe in, God's promise to perfect and complete the work He has begun in your life? Now, while God is faithfully doing His work, here's what He asks of you:

✓ *Be encouraged...*by God's promise of completion. Take heart that God is not finished with you. You are "a work in progress." And as an unfinished project, you have areas with specific needs.

What are your specific needs? Mentally list them. Spiritually pray about them. Practically be encouraged. God is at work in your life, and He will perfect and complete what He has begun regardless of any obstacles, failures, or speed bumps that come along the way.

✓ *Be growing*...as you participate in God's promise of completion. You are to...

> **C** onfess your sin (1 John 1:9).

> **O** bey God's Word (1 Thessalonians 2:13).

> **M** ake every effort to walk in God's ways (Ephesians 4:1).

> **P** lan to grow in grace and knowledge (2 Peter 3:18).

> **L** earn how to better run the Christian race to win (1 Corinthians 9:24).

> **E** nlist the help of other Christians (Hebrews 10:24).

> **T** ake time out for church each week (Hebrews 10:25).

> **E** valuate your progress regularly (Galatians 6:4).

✓ *Be confident*...in God's promise of completion. At one time or another, I have turned to others for help in gaining confidence for speaking in front of an audience. But, friend, for everything in life, both you and I should have the greatest confidence in God—a confidence that cannot be exceeded. We can be confident that our life and eternal destiny are fully in the hands of an all-powerful God, who does not leave anything to chance. He loves you unconditionally, and He will ensure that what He has started in your life will be completed.

If God is with us and we're with him,
we have nothing to fear.
Remember the promies of God,
and respond in faith.[7]

5

God's Powerful Promise of
Courage

I cannot remember when I first became interested in Civil War history. But I will testify that whenever I'm in one of my favorite haunts—a bookstore—it seems like I always gravitate toward books dealing with the clash between the northern and southern states in nineteenth-century America.

So, as usual, the last time I was in an airport, I made a beeline straight to the bookstore…and straight to the history section. There I found (and purchased!) a biography of one of the great—though controversial—generals of that war, Robert E. Lee.

As I began reading my new book on the next leg of my flight, I came across an account of Lee's adventures during another war, America's war with Mexico in 1846. This is how Lee's superior officer reported his performance during that conflict: "The greatest feat of physical and moral courage performed by any individual in my knowledge."[8]

It's no wonder that Robert E. Lee was such an influential person 15 years later during the Civil War. His courage inspired others to follow, even in the midst of overwhelming odds. This same courageous leadership was instantly evident when Lee lead the Army of Virginia into victory at the first major battle of the Civil War at Manassas.

Discovering the Promise

Before Robert E. Lee's time, there was another general who ultimately had the courage needed to win the victory. That general's name was Joshua, and you can read his story in the book of the Bible that bears his name. In the beginning of his leadership of God's people, the Israelites, Joshua appears to be somewhat fearful and anxious. That's understandable because...

> Joshua was following in the sandals of the bigger-than-life Moses, the same Moses who talked to God and who had lead the people out of Egypt. Then there was...
>
> Joshua's army, if you could call it that! His men were a ragtag band with little or no military training and experience in battle. And finally, there was...
>
> Joshua's enemy who inhabited the land. Joshua had seen them himself. They were giants, of savage tribes who refused to give up their land without a fierce fight (Numbers 13:32; 14:45).

God must have recognized some degree of fear in His general. How else can we explain the repeated attempts by the Lord to comfort and encourage His new leader? During one of God's "pep talks," He said to Joshua,

> *Be strong and courageous!...*
> *For the LORD your God is with you*
> *wherever you go.*
> JOSHUA 1:9

This exhortation from God was not an empty attempt to bolster Joshua's courage. Embedded in God's admonishment to Joshua was a promise to back up the reason to "be strong and courageous": The Lord Himself would be with him wherever he went!

Understanding the Promise

As we come to this powerful promise that's available to every Christian, we are shown three reasons Joshua did not need to be afraid. And these same three reasons are also why you can be courageous in fighting the battles you face in life.

1. *Courage grows from God's character.*

God said to Joshua, "Be strong and courageous." He was like a coach on the sidelines, encouraging Joshua to "lead these people to victory—give them the land!"

"Why, Lord?" we might wonder.

Because "I swore to their fathers to give them possession of the land," explains God (Joshua 1:6). End of discussion! God promised it...and it was as good as done.

As we have—and will—note throughout this book, God's nature will not allow Him to go back on His promises. Joshua could go into battle with courage, knowing that God had promised victory. God was not going to allow him to fail.

I personally believe God's reassurance of His promise to Joshua should give every Christian confidence. God has promised you the victory. Do you believe that? Then trust God. "Thanks be to God, who always leads us in His triumph in Christ" (2 Corinthians 2:14). That's a promise! Again, what confidence we can have in the battles we face and fight in life! Let's face them with God's promised courage.

2. *Courage expands with God's guidance.*

Maybe Joshua was still wavering. Maybe Joshua wasn't quite sure he wanted the job. (You can probably relate!) Whatever it was, God told him again, "Be strong and very courageous" (Joshua 1:7). In essence, God coached, "Take even more courage, Joshua!" Why? "Because I have given you the battle plans that will guide you to success!" God gave Joshua guidance, and He gives it to you, too, through His Word. So...

> Be careful to do according to all the law which Moses My servant commanded you (verse 7).

Some years ago I heard of a good football team that was defeated by a weaker team. It didn't matter what play was run—the opponent seemed to know exactly how to defend against the play. The coaches on the stronger team were mystified as they tried to make sense of their loss. Then, sometime later, the mystery was solved: One of their playbooks had gotten into the hands of the opposing team. The stolen playbook gave the opposing team a guide to victory. They knew every play the other team might possibly attempt.

God has given us, as Christians, a playbook as well—the Bible. This means we can make a successful defense against the "flaming missiles of the evil one" (Ephesians 6:16). So purpose to follow God's advice to Joshua. Don't get distracted and lose your courage. Don't turn to the right or to the left. Keep your devotion focused on God and His playbook for your life "so that you may have success wherever you go" (Joshua 1:7).

3. Courage multiplies with God's presence.

We'll spend time reveling in the power of God's presence later in this book. But log this well: God promised to be with Joshua *wherever* he went. For the third and final time, God declared to His leader, "Be strong and courageous." And then God added, "Do not tremble or be dismayed." Why? "For the LORD your God is with you wherever you go" (Joshua 1:9).

I'm sure you have faced a difficult situation, or had a meeting or a rigorous commitment you needed to brave, or played in a "big game" or match in which you really needed to perform well. We've all been there, haven't we? And how encouraging it is when you have family and friends nearby to support and encourage you! Their presence provides a stimulus for you to do your best, or the courage for you to do the right thing.

Well, it's even more motivating to know that *God* is always right there with you, no matter what happens...and no matter where you go. This was Joshua's secret to his courage. And friend, it should be yours, too, as you make your way through life's challenges.

Putting God's Power to Work

Is your courage a little thin these days? Do you feel like you are being overwhelmed by tough encounters and responsibilities? Take courage, my newfound friend. God is *with you*, to help you fight your battles. Be strong and courageous!

✓ *Remember*...to read your Bible daily. Ask God to guide you as you heed His instruction. His Word is a lamp to your feet and a light to your path (Psalm 119:105).

✓ *Remember*...God is not looking for soldiers to fight physical and political battles like those waged by General Lee. No, God is looking for those with the courage to fight daily battles on the spiritual plane. He's looking for spiritual soldiers—like you—who possess the courage to...

> ... stand up for Christ in public, at work, and at home.

> ... model godly character to others.

> ... fulfill your role in your family.

> ... guide your family out of worldliness and into godliness.

> ... speak up for morality at your children's school.

> ... live a consistent life for Christ, regardless of the cost.

✓ *Remember*...if you are feeling anxious or afraid about something today, or your courage is faltering, go ahead and do what Joshua did: Draw power and courage from...

> God's character,

> > God's Word, and

> > > God's presence.

*Since God is with you and you are with God,
you have nothing to fear!*

In our own strength we may often fail,
but in the power of Christ
we can conquer temptation and
live on the victory side![9]

6

God's Powerful Promise of
Deliverance

L iving for 30 years in Southern California with the constant threat of earthquakes has made me a bit cautious whenever I go into buildings. And this wariness was especially acute right after the 6.8-magnitude killer earthquake in Northridge, California—the epicenter of which was only three miles from my home. Even today, several years after that quake, as I enter a building, I immediately look for the exit signs. I instinctively wonder, *Where are they?* And, *What is the quickest way to get to them?* I'm not paranoid (or am I?). I must still be looking for the "big one"!

Discovering the Promise

Now, you may never have to contend with earthquakes,

but what about your last plane trip? What was the first thing the flight attendants told you? They instructed you on how to exit the plane during an emergency, didn't they? Exit routes are very important to know, whether for fire safety, plane mishaps, earthquake survival...or even when dealing with temptation.

Temptation comes into every believer's life. Not one of us is immune (and you know what I'm talking about!). Well, how would you like a promise for victory over temptation? Friend, this is what God wants to do for you!

> *No temptation has overtaken you*
> *but such as is common to man;*
> *and God is faithful,*
> *who will not allow you to be tempted*
> *beyond what you are able,*
> *but with the temptation will provide*
> *the way of escape also,*
> *that you may be able to endure it.*
> 1 CORINTHIANS 10:13

In these reassuring words, God promises you deliverance from sin. In other words, this is God's promise of an "exit." God isn't showing us *how* to exit our dangerous situations. No, He is showing us how *He* will provide an exit so we won't succumb to life's temptations.

So, friend, we should not view temptation as a bad thing. It is neither bad nor good. It is simply an opportunity for us to reaffirm and strengthen our faith and trust in God.

And here's another important fact: Temptation should not be viewed as sin. Rather, *giving in* to a temptation is sin!

In the past, I worked out regularly in a gym. My strength developed as I put tension on my muscles. The more I allowed the weights to produce tension on my physical muscles, the stronger they became. Temptation, when resisted, can help build our spiritual muscles much like the iron weights in the gym build up physical muscles—the more we can hold out against temptation, the stronger our spiritual muscles become. So it's vital for us to resist temptation as much as we can.

But what if the temptation gets too heavy for us to bear? This is where God's promise of deliverance comes to our rescue and saves the day. Going back to my experiences in the gym: If a man was doing a heavy workout, he had a "spot man" present to help him in case the weights got too heavy. Well, I guess you could say that God is the "spot man" for us, male or female. He's not a spectator in our lives. He's actively involved and ever present. He wants to help. And when temptations become too heavy to handle on our own, He delivers us by making a way of escape, by providing an escape route, an exit out of the temptation.

How does God's promise of deliverance work?

Understanding the Promise

1. *Deliverance involves the character of God.*

We should never become disturbed or discouraged when a temptation comes our way. We are not alone or unique when it comes to enticements. As one writer noted, "If you are alive, you are tempted."[10] But there is hope! *God is faithful.* God, by His very nature, will not leave us alone to face Satan and our own sinfulness. Instead, He is present with us as we face temptation, and hopefully, by His grace, we will resist it.

2. *Deliverance does not remove temptation.*

Now, God doesn't always remove the temptation. Facing the

temptation and remaining strong can strengthen and give maturity to your Christian life. But God does promise He will keep the temptation from becoming too strong for you to handle. He "will not allow you to be tempted beyond what you are able...that you may be able to endure it." Temptation can be resisted because God says you can "endure it."

3. Deliverance provides a way of escape.

God promises us the strength to endure temptation. He also promises to "provide the way of escape" from temptation. Whether we endure or escape, we are to be actively resisting temptation. We are also to be looking for the exit in any and every difficult situation. God's "way of escape" requires us to be on the lookout for His deliverance...and counting on it!

And friend, the way out is not always easy. In fact, many times it is the harder road. That's why so many people give in to temptation. It's easier than waiting for a way out.

What will "the way to escape" look like? God's deliverance may arrive through any number of avenues, whether it's people or, at times, just plain ol' common sense. Whatever it is, or whoever it is that God uses to provide the way of escape, don't fail to head for the exit. Your spiritual life is dependent on it!

Meet a man who failed to resist temptation. The sad story of David, the king of Israel, is told in 2 Samuel 11. He had everything he wanted or needed. What toppled this mighty warrior and leader of God's people? He stopped depending on God's strength when...

> —temptation came. David "saw a woman bathing, and the woman was very beautiful in appearance" (verse 2).

—temptation progressed to sin in thought. David lingered long enough in his gaze to begin lusting after this very beautiful woman, and he then took another step into sin and "inquired about the woman" (verse 3).

—temptation progressed to sin in deed. "David sent messengers and took her...[and] he lay with her" (verse 4).

The tragedy is that David could have been delivered from sin. He could have chosen not to look...and the temptation would have passed. Or, David could have cried out to the Lord for strength to resist and been delivered. David is a classic example of someone who did not want or look for a way of escape and, therefore, did not resist temptation.

Meet a man who successfully resisted temptation. Joseph is a man every Christian should look to as a role model because he resisted temptation.

—temptation came. In Joseph's case, the woman came after him. She said, "Lie with me" (Genesis 39:7). And this wasn't a one-time offer. Oh, no! "She spoke to Joseph *day after day*" (verse 10).

—temptation was resisted. How?

Joseph *valued* loyalty to others above his own personal gratification. He told the aggressive woman, *"My master*...has put all that he owns in my charge....he has withheld nothing from me except you" (verse 8).

Joseph *viewed* the temptation for what it was, a "great evil" (verse 9). Temptation disguises itself as something beautiful, something that is rightfully yours, something that will be fun and pleasurable. Once someone begins to view temptation through rose-colored glasses, it's not long before that person takes the next step, gives in to the temptation, and commits the sin.

Joseph *voiced* the connection between his actions and his relationship with God. "How could I do this great evil, and *sin against God?*" (verse 9). Joseph knew that his actions affected his relationship with a holy God. Yes, others may be involved, but for a believer, sin is ultimately an issue with God!

Joseph was under tremendous daily pressure and temptation on the job. But he *resisted and fled* for the exit...literally (verse 12)! He provides us with God's model for dealing with our temptations. So the next time you are in the midst of a temptation, ask yourself, "Which model will I follow—David, or Joseph?"

Putting God's Power to Work

It can't be said enough—everyone, even strong leaders such as David and Joseph, faces temptation! And you will face temptation, too. But pause for a moment and think about God's powerful promise to deliver you from sin. That doesn't mean you will never sin. But it does mean God is available to help you resist temptation so you don't sin. He is with you to protect you from unbearable temptation by always giving you a way out.

Now, your responsibility is to discern where the exit is, and how to get there. Here are some things to think about—some ways of escape, if you will—as you count on God for His promise of deliverance.

✓   *Realize*...that temptation confronts everyone.

✓ *Recognize*...that temptation often comes disguised as a shortcut, an easy way out, a better life, a pretty girl or handsome guy, a zeal for success, a get-rich-quick scheme, a bigger and better house.

✓ *Remember*...those people and places that give you the greatest temptation. Avoid compromising situations.

✓ *Run*...from areas of weakness.

✓ *Rely*...on God's help. Pray before you act. Prayer shows your dependence on God and also helps keep you from acting in a rash or foolish way.

✓ *Read*...God's Word. Find out what He says about resisting temptation.

✓ *Reason*...through the consequences. How will you and those close to you be affected by your actions?

✓ *Recruit*...other Christians who can support you when you are tempted.

✓ *Rejoice*...that temptation can be resisted. God is the Great Deliverer!

God has cast our confessed sins
into the depths of the sea,
and He's even put a "No Fishing"
sign over the spot.
—DWIGHT L. MOODY

7

God's Powerful Promise of
Forgiveness

C hristmas is a festive and joyous time of the year. And, as your joint checking account will testify, gift-giving is a prominent element of the holiday season!

If you're like me, you probably received a few gifts that you aren't sure what to do with. Perhaps your Aunt Mabel gave you a sweater that doesn't fit, and it isn't even a color that looks good on you. And what about that bottle of after-shave or perfume? Wow! The odor was so strong that the flowers at work wilted when you walked by. Gifts like these were given by well-meaning friends and family, but you probably saved the original boxes so you could return them as soon as possible!

But what about those "perfect" gifts from loved ones that were ideal for you and even useful? You wore that shirt or that robe until it became a rag! And you're still using that power tool or food mixer.

Friend, God has given you an even more cherished and useful gift—a life-saving one! He gave the gift of His Son, the Lord Jesus Christ. The apostle Paul called God's gift of Jesus "His indescribable gift" (2 Corinthians 9:15).

Discovering the Promise

When you receive God's gift of Jesus, you also receive the benefit of our next powerful promise—the promise of God's forgiveness. God's forgiveness is so complete that He promises that...

> *As far as the east is from the west,*
> *so far has He removed our*
> *transgressions from us.*
> PSALM 103:12

Are you struggling with any sin you think is too big for God to forgive? Remember that God is bigger than all your sin. Sure, there may be an aftermath you will have to deal with in your life. Broken relationships are hard to mend, broken laws have their just penalties, borrowed and mismanaged money must be repaid. But God's cleansing love and forgiveness will see you through any and all consequences.

How about the other end of the sin-spectrum? Maybe you think your sin is too small for God to care about or notice—you know, those "little white lies," those careless acts of indiscretion. You may be wishfully thinking these little sins are so small that they are "undetectable" on God's radar screen. Or possibly that they have a "statute of limitation" with God. Someday they will just...go away.

But these unconfessed sins do have a consequence. They hinder your fellowship with a holy and just God. It's true that God forgives sin, but it's also true He overlooks none. So whether your sins are big or small, you need to experience God's promise of forgiveness for them. Now, what is involved in this forgiveness?

Understanding the Promise

1. *God's forgiveness is complete.*

It's important to note that when you receive Jesus Christ and are born into the family of God, your sins are forgiven once and for all. When Jesus uttered, "It is finished" on the cross, He was speaking of His work of redemption (John 19:30). Jesus died for your sins and mine. Every sin that you and I will ever commit is covered by Jesus' death.

Christian, as God's child, His forgiveness is complete because Jesus' work is complete. God's justice was satisfied when His Son died. God can therefore show His mercy and complete forgiveness to you.

2. *God's forgiveness is permanent.*

You can probably still remember a hurtful deed someone did to you in the past. Maybe you have forgiven that person of that wrong, and you are trying to forget it. But the pain is still there, and it keeps popping into your memory.

God is not like you and your memories. When God forgives, He also forgets...which is exactly what our powerful promise states: "As far as the east is from the west, so far has He removed our transgressions." Read how one teacher explains this promise of forgiveness:

The sins of believers shall be remembered no more, shall not be mentioned unto them; they shall be sought for, and not found. If we thoroughly forsake them, God will thoroughly forgive them.[11]

3. God's forgiveness is unending.

God's gift of forgiveness is the "gift that keeps on giving." You can't use up God's forgiveness. Whether your sins are few or many, whether they are big or small, God will always be there to forgive. While God's ability to continually forgive doesn't give you license to deliberately mess up, it's encouraging to know God is always ready to forgive. (And we follow in His steps when we forgive each other.)

4. God's forgiveness is to be shared.

One of the greatest blessings of God's forgiveness to us is the opportunity to pass that same mercy on to others (Matthew 5:7). God has forgiven you so much! Shouldn't you do the same for others?

How often and how much should you forgive another person? Jesus answered, "Seventy times seven" (Matthew 18:22). In other words, your forgiveness should be limitless.

Forgiveness toward others is an identifying mark of a believer. Forgiveness from God is man's deepest need, but forgiveness of others is man's highest achievement. And such forgiveness should begin in your home, toward those who are closest to you.

5. God's forgiveness changes us.

It's wonderful that God's forgiveness is complete, permanent, and limitless. But let's make the most of each act of forgiveness on God's part. Let's treat them as opportunities to learn a lesson... such as how to avoid the same sin in the future! Of course, we should *ask God for forgiveness*. He wants us to admit, as quickly as possible, when we have done wrong. But let's go a step further and also *ask God for wisdom*. Let's also constantly seek advice in God's Word and from godly Christian friends. Let's change, let's grow in our Christian walk, let's learn to avoid sin!

Putting God's Power to Work

Are you wondering, *Will God still forgive me if I make the same mistake?* Answer: Absolutely! But you should make it your constant goal to grow from your mistakes and learn from God's wonderful forgiveness. How?

- ✓ *Prayerfully*...thank God for His complete forgiveness of the wrongs you have committed in the past. Accept God's forgiveness, embrace His mercy, and trust in His powerful promise that He has forgiven you in Jesus Christ. What a Savior!

- ✓ *Purposefully*...remember every day that God has forgiven your sins in Jesus. Remember the promise—He has removed your sins as far away as the east is from the west. That's as far away as you can get! The two shall never meet.

- ✓ *Purposefully*...forget what has happened in the past and joyously follow God's plans for your life, full steam ahead! You have a clean slate, a life with second chances. No one can give you that but God!

✓ *Prayerfully*...make a list of the people you need to forgive, the people who have wronged you. Begin with the
person closest to you. Now that you have experienced
God's forgiveness, you should be able to extend it to
him or her and to others. Pray through the list. Ask God
to help you forgive each person without any lingering
resentment. Forgiveness is a two-way street. A "forgiven
soul" is a "forgiving soul."

✓ *Prayerfully*...make a list of the people *you* have wronged.
What are your plans for making things right? Will you go
to them? Call them? When? And what will you say? What
will your first step be?

✓ *Praise*...God constantly for His indescribable gift. Again,
Jesus is the gift that keeps on giving. Be sure to share the
good news of His forgiveness with others.

✓ *Put away bitterness*...toward others. It poisons your
heart and your relationships (Hebrews 12:15). It just isn't
worth it!

✓ *Put on a heart of forgiveness*...and "be kind to one
another, tender-hearted, forgiving each other, just as God
in Christ also has forgiven you" (Ephesians 4:32).

Grace is not sought nor bought nor wrought.
It is a free gift of Almighty God
to needy mankind.
—Billy Graham

8

God's Powerful Promise of
Grace

Grace. Just say the word, and many think immediately of the Christian hymn "Amazing Grace." And, truly, the story of the writer of this hymn is all about the amazing grace of God.

John Newton was a slave trader who plied his business in the 1800s. He was a rough and immoral man who later described himself as a "wretch"—which, from all accounts, he was...and more! Through a set of severe, life-threatening circumstances, Newton experienced a dramatic conversion that changed his heart and his way of life. He went on to become both a famous preacher and songwriter. No wonder the first line of his hymn marvels, "Amazing grace, how sweet the sound that saved a wretch like me!"[12]

Discovering God's Promise

As you learn about God's grace, feel free to hum along with me or even sing John Newton's great hymn as we walk our way through another incredible promise from God, the powerful promise of His grace—for the grace of God is truly *amazing!* In fact, God says...

> *My grace is sufficient for you.*
> 2 CORINTHIANS 12:9

Have you ever done something bad—*really* bad? You knew you were wrong, and so did everyone else. And yet, your spouse, or your boss, or your children forgave you? Then you've tasted a little of what it means to receive mercy that was not warranted. That's what God's grace is! Simply put, "grace" is God's mercy, God's favor—God's *unmerited* favor.

From the very beginning of recorded history, God has demonstrated His favor, starting with Adam and Eve. This couple willfully disobeyed God and deserved the punishment of death for their disobedience. But God showed forth His grace—His favor—toward them instead, which was definitely unmerited!

And so it has been down through Bible history. The nation of Israel is another example of God's grace. The people deserved destruction, but God was gracious. Hear Nehemiah's prayer of thanksgiving to God for His grace—His unmerited favor—to the nation of Israel:

> Nevertheless, in Thy great compassion Thou didst not make an end of them or forsake them, for Thou art a gracious and compassionate God (Nehemiah 9:31).

Understanding the Promise

1. *God's grace saves.*

Now let's fast-forward to today, to you and to me. The Bible clearly states that "all [and that "all" means all!] have sinned and fall short of the glory of God" (Romans 3:23), and that "the wages of sin is death" (Romans 6:23). Like all those who have gone before us, we don't deserve God's favor, either. We deserve death. But (and here comes God's undeserved favor), "by grace you have been saved through faith; and that not of yourselves, it is a gift of God" (Ephesians 2:8).

Grace is God's intentional bestowal of His loving favor on those whom He saves. We can't earn grace. If we could, it would no longer be unmerited. And we cannot save ourselves. Only God can save us. The only way for us to receive this gift of God's grace is by faith in Jesus Christ (Romans 3:24).

Friend, has God's grace been poured out on you through Jesus Christ? If so, then you have experienced God's amazing, sufficient, and undeserved grace.

2. *God's grace guides.*

Like John Newton, the apostle Paul was a despicable character before he met Jesus on the Damascus Road (Acts 9:1-9). He came to Jesus with a past. He had persecuted and killed Christians. Yet even with his stained past, Paul could say,

> By the grace of God I am what I am, and His grace toward me did not prove vain; but I labored even more than all of them, yet not I, but the grace of God with me (1 Corinthians 15:10).

God's grace reached down and changed Paul's life so completely that he went from being a Christian-hater to being a

Christian who loved his brothers and sisters in Christ. And Paul recognized it was God's grace that changed him, and it was God's grace that shaped and molded and ultimately guided him over his 20-plus years as a believer.

Have you experienced a time in the past (or maybe even now) when you were trying to control your own life, to steer your own boat, to set the sails of your own destiny?

There was a time when I tried to be the captain of my own life. But God, in His great grace, stepped in, intervened, and took control. And every time I look back on the path my life has taken, I see the goodness God has had in mind as He worked out what was best for me.

So how is it going for you? Do you want God's guidance? Do you want to live a life of no regrets? Do you want to enjoy a life that can declare, along with the apostle Paul, "I am what I am...[by] His grace"?

If so (and why wouldn't you), then you must give your life over to God's guidance. Like Paul, you must constantly ask, "What shall I do, Lord?" (Acts 22:10). With this question, you, like Paul, are seeking God's grace and guidance in your life. Do you ever need help? God's grace can guide you!

3. God's grace empowers.

The Christian life is not always a bed of roses. In fact, the Bible says that "all who desire to live godly in Christ Jesus will be persecuted" (2 Timothy 3:12). (How's that for a promise?) So we can pretty much count on facing at least some persecution. And besides that, there are the heartaches that come with life and living—the loss of a baby or a family member, the loss of a job or health, the pain of difficult circumstances or financial problems. So how do we cope with these? How do we gain the victory?

The answer, again, is God's grace.

The apostle Paul had a tough problem. We don't know if what he labeled as his "thorn in the flesh" was a physical ailment or a person, but something or someone was there to "torment" Paul (2 Corinthians 12:7 NIV). It bothered him enough that he asked God three times to take it away (verse 8). And what was God's response to Paul? God promised, "My gracious favor is all you need" (verse 9 NLT).

God's promise of power through His grace caused Paul to turn a corner and proclaim, "Most gladly, therefore, I will rather boast about my weaknesses, that the power of Christ may dwell in me" (verse 9).

God's promised grace is truly amazing. In addition to being limitless...

—God's grace is sufficient for your salvation.

—God's grace is sufficient to shape and mold you into the person you need to be to serve your family, your church, and your world.

—God's grace is sufficient to see you through any trial you will ever face or any need you will ever experience.

—God's grace is truly sufficient for anything the world might throw at you. Anything! (And that's the bottom line!)

—God's grace will be sufficient to see you home to glory. (Now that's the best news of all!)

Putting God's Power to Work

It's an understatement to say that the Christian life is not easy. In fact, you could say that it is impossible. You, like Paul, will experience weaknesses, insults, distresses, persecution, and difficulties (2 Corinthians 12:10). But take cheer! God promises that when you allow His grace to control you in your difficulties, He will give you a strength that will empower you through the myriad of problems that will come your way. God has—and will—continue to do His part. Now, what can you do to put God's promise of G-R-A-C-E to work in your life?

G ive thanks...to God that you are under grace and not the law.

R espond...in love and obedience to the gift of God's grace in your life.

A sk God...for wisdom to understand what His grace should mean in your life.

C ommune...with other believers in a Bible-teaching church where you can receive training in the ways of God's grace.

E xtend God's grace...to others by

sharing the gospel

showing forgiveness, and

shouldering their burdens.

He who trusts his own wisdom
to guide him through life
is a fool.
He is casting his anchor inside the boat,
and thus will drift incessantly.
The one who looks to the Lord for
guidance acts wisely.[13]

9

God's Powerful Promise of
Guidance

Over the years I have made a serious commitment to keep in shape by jogging. On occasion, this decision has presented its own set of unique problems. For instance, the time I was jogging in Paris, France. While I was there visiting a missionary friend and his family, I decided to get up early before our meetings began and go for a run. It was a glorious spring day, the kind Paris is famous for. So off I went.

As I ran, I sort of paid attention to my surroundings. But then, as I usually do when I'm running, I got lost in my thoughts. I always run for a specific number of minutes, so that morning, when half of my allotted time was up, I turned around to head back to my friend's apartment building. But to my surprise, when I did my about-face, nothing looked familiar! It was still very early in the morning, so only a few people were out. And the street signs and storefronts were in French...of which I did not know even one word to use in asking for help. Basically, I was lost in Paris!

"How did you get back to the apartment?" you ask. Well, at first I told myself that if I ran around for a while, eventually I would see a familiar sight and would then know how to make my way back. But after basically running around in circles for some time, nothing was looking even remotely familiar! It was then I began to get very nervous. Why hadn't I thought to bring my friend's address, or at least his phone number? I had even left my passport at the apartment. And if I didn't get out of this mess soon, I could see myself lost forever on the streets of Paris!

Friend, when all else fails, pray. Now, isn't that usually the way it goes? I didn't think of praying until I was about ready to push the panic button. "Lord," I asked, "please show me something that will help guide me back to the apartment."

Was it "coincidence," or answered prayer? (I think you know the answer!) Almost before I could finish my cry to God, I saw it—the Talbot truck showroom sign. Why had the sign made such an impression? It wasn't because I'm familiar with foreign trucks. Actually, I had never heard of the Talbot Truck Company. No, *Talbot* is the name of the seminary where I received my theological training. And for that reason I had made a special note of the showroom when I passed by it. Within ten minutes, I was safely back at the apartment.

Discovering the Promise

Have you ever had a similar experience? Were you lost and in need of directions? Or were you in the midst of serious decision-making and needed guidance? Well, God has a promise just for you!

> *Trust in the Lord with all your heart,*
> *and do not lean on your own understanding.*
> *In all your ways acknowledge Him,*
> *and He will make your paths straight.*
> PROVERBS 3:5-6

Take note: In this promise from God, He does not guarantee that any one of us won't get lost on the streets of Paris or any other city. But He does promise to give us a lifetime of guidance...if we want it.

Understanding the Promise

One thousand years before Jesus came to earth, King Solomon gave his understanding of what is needed in order to receive guidance from God. As you have already read in this chapter's promise, Solomon said we must choose God's path and allow Him to guide us. So how is it that we obtain God's promised guidance? We must...

1. *Depend on God completely.*

In other words, "trust in the Lord with all your heart." Rely totally upon God's wisdom. God knows what is best for you, your endeavors, and your future. He created you. Therefore He is a better judge (than you are) of the direction your life should take. You must trust and obey God's direction completely, regardless of how painful it is to do so. The word *trust* literally means "to lie helpless, facedown." "It pictures either a servant waiting for his master's command in readiness to obey, or a defeated soldier yielding himself to the conquering general."[14]

2. *Regard your own wisdom lightly.*

If you are really honest with yourself, you will judge your ability to make wise and godly decisions as hit-and-miss at best. The Bible cautions, "Do not be wise in your own eyes" (Proverbs 3:7). But let's quickly agree together that God has given us a measure of wisdom. You can, and hopefully do, think carefully about the decisions you make. But God also cautions us not to think so highly of our personal thoughts that we make decisions based solely on our wisdom. So be careful not to exclude other sources of wisdom that God makes available to you. Wisdom can come from the Bible, from wise leaders at church, and from godly counselors. God's Word and wise people should be consulted in order to make the best and wisest decisions possible.

3. *Seek God's will always.*

To receive God's guidance, Solomon said, "In all your ways acknowledge Him." In other words, you are to seek God's will in all that you do. This means you are to...

—Turn every area of your life over to God. Jesus put it this way: "Seek first His kingdom and His righteousness" (Matthew 6:33). Are there any matters you have not turned over to God's wise control?

—Examine your values and priorities. What is important to you? Do your priorities and values match up with God's?

When you determine to acknowledge God's presence and include Him in all that you do, be assured, "He will make your paths straight." He will guide you into accomplishing His purposes and not your own. We will become more like the Master and be able to say, "Not My will, but Thine be done" (Luke 22:42).

Putting God's Power to Work

Now let's roll up our sleeves and put this powerful promise to work! How have you been making your decisions? By trial and error? By hit and miss? By guess and by golly? Well, it's time for that to change. The next time you need guidance, follow this to-do and not-to-do list. It will help direct you right into the will of God!

✓   *Do not...*under any circumstances, rely solely on your own reason. Why? Because "he who trusts in his own heart is a fool" (Proverbs 28:26). Consult God and others.

✓   *Do*...acknowledge the need for God's guidance in all decisions, great *and* small. It's "the little foxes" that can give you the biggest problems and lead to the greatest disasters (Song of Solomon 2:15). Don't minimize the need for guidance, especially in the seemingly small decisions.

✓   *Do*...listen to and be corrected by God's Word and wise counselors. Welcome advice. A fool is wise only in his own eyes (Proverbs 12:15)!

✓   *Do*...use your God-given ability to think through issues and options. And remember, thinking takes time—time alone with God.

✓   *Do*...be patient until God's will becomes perfectly clear. Realize that the path that leads to God's will is well marked (Proverbs 15:19) and well lit (Proverbs 4:18). Beware of paths that are poorly marked and not well lit.

✓ *Do...* pray over every decision as if it's the most important decision you will ever make because you never know—it just might be! Your life is affected by every decision you make.

My hope is built on nothing less
Than Jesus' blood and righteousness;
I dare not trust the sweetest frame,
But wholly lean on Jesus' name.[15]

10

God's Powerful Promise of Hope

I am hoping and praying that this is not true about you, but sadly, most people don't know what they are reaching for in life. They don't know their purpose. So what do they do? They fixate on wealth, power, relationships, and health. They believe that achievement in these spheres will satisfy their inner longings.

But do such conquests really accomplish that? Are people truly happy when they achieve fitness, finances, influence, and friendships?

The answer is *yes* to some extent. But friend, there is more— so much more—to life! As one miserable man wrote in his suicide note, "I am worth ten million dollars as men judge things, but I am so poor in spirit that I cannot live any longer. Something is terribly wrong with life."

What, we wonder, was missing from this man's life?

In a word...*hope!* Have you heard this saying? "You can live 40 days without food, five minutes without air, but you can't live even one second without hope." Real hope, a confident hope, is what people—even that wealthy, successful businessman—are longing for. But they make the mistake of looking for it in all the wrong places.

Discovering the Promise

True and lasting hope is revealed in only one place—the Bible. True and lasting hope is found in only one person—Jesus Christ. And true and lasting hope is promised from only one source—God! Hear now one of His many powerful promises of hope:

> *"For I know the plans that I have for you,"*
> *declares the* Lord,
> *"plans for welfare and not for calamity*
> *to give you a future and a hope."*
> Jeremiah 29:11

"Which do you want first, the good news or the bad news?" How many times have you heard that question? And how do you usually respond? Do you ask for the good news first, or the bad?

Well, in the case of God's promise of hope in Jeremiah 29:11, God first gave His people some bad news. He informed the children of Israel they would remain in captivity away from their homeland for 70 years as punishment for repeatedly failing to follow His commands (verse 10).

But on the heels of the bad news came good news: At the end of their 70 years in exile, God would once again visit His people and fulfill His promise to return them to their land. This was great news of hope.

Understanding the Promise

Seventy years is a l-o-n-g time! Imagine how easy it would be for the people to lose hope and assume that God had turned His back on them. Imagine how often they may have been tempted—perhaps daily!—to think that God no longer loved them or cared about them. But all such thoughts would definitely be incorrect! So to prevent such wrong thinking, God gave the Israelites this shining promise of hope through His prophet Jeremiah.

Oh, did Israel ever need to be encouraged! They needed to know that in spite of their situation they could still be firmly rooted in their trust in God and their belief in God's loving concern for them. Yes, they had sinned and disobeyed God repeatedly. But God was giving them *hope* that, even in the midst of their *calamity,* He was working out His *plans* for their lives and their *future.*

And, fellow Christian, God is working out His plan for your life as well. You, like the Israelites, can have confidence in God's plan for you. Why can you have such steadfast hope? Because your hope is not like a ship that is at the mercy of the changing winds. No, your hope is anchored in God Himself!

1. *Hope is grounded in God's power.*

Do you ever think about the fact that God knows, in advance, everything that will happen? That's because He is the author of history—including your history. You are a part of His grand plan—" 'I know the plans that I have for you,' declares the LORD." Because He knows the future, and has designed your personal agenda, and is present with you, you can have boundless hope—a hope grounded in the promise of an all-powerful God. The stronger your faith in God is, the stronger your hope will be!

2. *Hope is strengthened by God's good plan.*

When something terrible happens in your life, are you ever tempted to ask, "What good could come out of this?" It *looks* like a disaster. Furthermore, it *feels* like a disaster. Therefore you quickly conclude, "It *is* a disaster!"

It's then you must remember God's powerful promise, "I know the plans that I have for you...they are plans for good and not for disaster" (NLT).

When the Israelites were punished for 70 years, to them it may have appeared, at first glance, that God was finished with them. After all, He had allowed their country to be destroyed and them to be sent into exile. This must have looked like a disaster! *What good,* they may have wondered, *could come out of this?*

But God did not forget His people who were suffering in Babylon.

And, my friend, He won't forget you! God had a plan—a beautiful plan—to turn His people into a beautiful new people, with a beautiful new purpose. And He promises to do the same for you. God had a plan that had His people's welfare in mind... and the same is true of His plan for you!

Once again, no matter what is happening in your life, you must always remember God's powerful promise, "I know the plans that I have for you…they are plans for good and not for disaster." And once again, God did not forget His people who were suffering in Babylon…and He won't forget you! God promised, and God delivered! And I repeat, He will do the same for you. He has a *plan* to take what seems like a disaster and, through His power and goodness, turn the situation into something grand and *good*.

Have you had any "disasters" lately? Does it appear that God has forgotten you? Think again! Strengthen yourself in the fact of God's goodness. He will use what appears to be a tragic circumstance to prepare you for greater spiritual growth and a renewed focus on Him. No price can be put on such blessings!

3. *Hope is energized through God's faithfulness.*

Do you ever have times when you stop for even a moment and revel in how faithful God has been in your life and, as a result, you are instantly energized to carry on, even in the midst of a bad situation? Such inspiring thoughts can surely encourage you to forge ahead, can't they?

Well, God did not want His people, the Israelites, to be discouraged. Had He not already faithfully taken care of them for hundreds of years through both good times as well as bad? And to God, their exile to Babylon was no different. He promised, "I will give you a future and a hope":

—*A future:* "I will bring you back to the place from where I sent you into exile" (Jeremiah 29:14).

—*A hope:* "Behold…I will make a new covenant with the house of Israel.…I will put My law within them, and on

their heart I will write it; and I will be their God, and
they shall be My people" (Jeremiah 31:31-33).

Won't you take a minute to stop and revel in how faithful
God has been to you up to this point? And while you're on
"pause," ponder the power of God's promise to you of...

—*A future:* "In My Father's house are many dwelling places...
    I go to prepare a place for you. And...I will come again,
    and receive you to Myself; that where I am, there you
    may be also" (John 14:2-3).

—*A hope:* God "shall dwell among [men and women] and
    they shall be His people and God Himself shall be
    among them" (Revelation 21:3).

Putting God's Power to Work

Corrie ten Boom, a prisoner in a Nazi concentration camp
during World War II and a woman who desperately needed
hope every minute of every day, made this statement: "Never
be afraid to trust an unknown future to a known God." Friend,
as a Christian, you don't need to act like those who have no
hope. Why? Because of Jesus Christ. Because of Him, you *know*
your future!

Please don't live a life of hopelessness! Don't get down or
depressed about the way things are going. And don't respond
to life's hardships with despair or self-indulgence. Instead,
unsheathe God's promise of hope when you feel despair
coming on, when your situation seems hopeless, when you
feel overwhelmed by the pressures of life and seeming injus-
tices. Grab hold of your hope, and fight against self-indulgence,
against giving in to anger, depression, sexual sin, overeating,

and any number of other defeating behaviors. Put God's powerful promise to work in these ways:

✓ *Recall*...God's promise of hope. Remember it often when you are discouraged.

✓ *Review*...God's words of hope and encouragement to you. To this point, we've looked at only *ten* of God's thousands of powerful promises! And each one of them is life-changing and loaded with hope! Which one do you like best so far?

✓ *Resist*...the temptation to give in to your flesh. Self-indulgence is for the hopeless, while self-control is for the hopeful. Choose the right response during trying times.

✓ *Rely on*...the God of hope. Trust in God's promise of hope. It's a promise and a hope founded on the rock-solid character of God.

✓ *Rejoice*...and thank God that you are the recipient of His powerful promise of hope. It will cheer up any dark days.

✓ *Recount*...God's track record of faithfulness. It's easy to look only at the dark days and forget the many bright days of God's blessings in your life.

✓ *Remember*...that no matter how bad things become, God has a plan—a plan for good—and that He will be with you in your every hour of need. He promises!

He who provides for this life,
but takes no care for eternity,
is wise for a moment,
but a fool forever.

Life with Christ
is an endless hope;
without Him
a hopeless end.[16]

11

God's Powerful Promise of Life

One of the prized gifts my parents gave me as a child was an interest in reading. At an early age my mother enrolled me in a children's classics book club. Every month the mailman brought a new classic...and I was off again, sailing with pirates on wind-driven ships and exploring uncharted islands in search of hidden treasure.

One tale that particularly fascinated me was the story about the search for the fountain of youth—you know, the spring whose waters supposedly had the power to restore youth. Believing this legend, Juan Ponce de León, a Spanish explorer, set out in 1513 on an expedition from Puerto Rico to discover this fountain whose life-giving powers were said to originate from an island called Bimini.

Needless to say, Ponce de León did not find the fountain of youth. But he did discover a land mass on Easter Sunday of 1513. He named the new territory *Pascua Florida*, which is Spanish for "flower of Easter." Today we have this explorer to thank for naming the state of Florida for us.

Discovering the Promise

This story of Juan Ponce de León points to the fascination people throughout time have had with life. Theirs is an obsession with life here and now and life in the hereafter. Such thoughts are constantly on every man and woman's mind, whether they verbalize it or not. Many ads on television offer new products that will make us look younger or feel more youthful. It appears people will spend almost any amount of money for "the fountain of youth." Yes, the preoccupation with life is permanently stamped on humanity.

But what if there was someone who could actually *give* you life? That would be terrific news, wouldn't it? Well, guess what: There *is* such a person, and His name is Jesus Christ. Listen to what God wants to do for you:

> *I came that [you] might have life,*
> *and might have it abundantly.*
> JOHN 10:10

We find these words in the apostle John's chronicle of the life of Jesus. In John's gospel, the theme of "life" is repeatedly emphasized. When you have the opportunity, read the book of John for yourself. You'll find he referred to life over 40 times! No other book of the Bible comes close to such a focus on life.

Are you interested in finding out more about the promise

of life offered by Jesus? Are you ready to do a little exploring? Then let's go!

Understanding the Promise

1. *Life is offered only by Jesus.*

Have you ever talked about why Jesus, God in flesh, came to this earth? Well, His promise gives you and me His purpose. Jesus came to offer life—abundant life and eternal life. Jesus said, "I came that they might have life, and might have it abundantly." He also proclaimed, "I give eternal life to them, and they shall never perish; and no one shall snatch them out of My hand" (John 10:28). Jesus is a giver of life—abundant life, and a sustainer of life—eternal life.

And to whom did Jesus offer eternal life? To those sheep who *hear* His voice and *follow* His leading (John 10:3). Are you one who has *heard* His voice and is *following* the Good Shepherd? If so, Jesus promises you will have life...and have it abundantly!

2. *Life is found only in Jesus.*

Philosophers and religious authorities from the beginning of recorded history have claimed that they know *a way* to God. Some of these authorities tell us there are "many roads that lead to God." But is that true? Only Jesus Christ could rightfully say, "I am *the way,* and *the truth,* and *the life;* no one comes to the Father, but through Me" (John 14:6).

People look everywhere for eternal life and end up missing the only one who can give it to them—Jesus, the God-Man! Which road are you taking? One of the many roads? Or are you on the only road? Being on the right road will determine whether you have life.

3. Life is abundant because of Jesus.

One of my sons-in-law is an astronomer. Paul has provided many exceptional stargazing sessions for our family by bringing his telescope to our home in the country on clear nights. Have you ever used a telescope that you could extend to increase its magnifying power? Well, my friend, life with Jesus is like such a telescope. Each time you pull out a new "section," life becomes larger, brighter, more enjoyable, and more fulfilling. That's what Jesus promises—"life in all its fullness" (John 10:10 NLT). Jesus promises...

- ~~~ Depth of living now—The life that Jesus gives you right now is abundantly rich and full. Just think about it: You have love, joy, peace, patience, kindness, goodness, faithfulness, gentleness, and self-control (Galatians 5:22-23). And let's not forget forgiveness and guidance. Is there anything missing? Not in Christ!

- ~~~ Length of living for eternity—Your eternal life starts the moment you accept Jesus' offer and embrace the Shepherd. As the saying goes, "This is the first day of the rest of your life." Since (I am hoping and praying!) you are already experiencing eternal life, how then should you live?

    —You should live expectantly. Your citizenship is in heaven (Philippians 3:20). Therefore, you are to live with the anticipation that the King will one day come to take you home.

    —You should live confidently. Ridicule and persecution may come. But as God's child, you can live with boldness. Why? Because nothing can separate you from your Shepherd (Romans 8:38-39).

Putting God's Power to Work

You have an eternal future. Your spiritual life began the moment you believed. Jesus Christ has given you an incredible gift. He has given you eternal life.

So what does it mean to possess eternal life? If you have received Christ, it means your life is not finished when you die physically. It's only just begun—you have life everlasting! How should the knowledge of this affect your life today?

✓ *Purpose*...to invite Christ into your heart and life *now* if you haven't already. You must *want* eternal life. It's a free gift, you know. And how does it become yours? John said, "As many as received Him, to them He gave the right to become children of God, even to those who believe in His name" (John 1:12). Have you received God's gift of eternal life? If not, or if you are unsure, you can pray a heartfelt prayer like this one. You can take this step toward Christ.

> Jesus, I want to follow You. I know that I am a sinner, and I want to repent of my sins. I believe You died for my sins and rose again victorious over the power of sin and death, and I want to accept You as my personal Savior. Come into my life, Lord Jesus, and help me follow and obey You from this day forward. Amen.

✓ *Purpose*...to live today with all your heart! You don't need to *wait* for eternal life. You have fellowship with God...today! *Today* is the first day of the rest of your life, and so is every day with Jesus!

✓ *Purpose*...to live today with a grateful heart. You don't need to *work* for eternal life. Christ has already done the work of salvation on your behalf. Have you thanked Him today?

✓ *Purpose*...to count on Jesus' promise and live with a heart of confidence today. You don't need to *worry* about losing eternal life. Note Jesus' words of promise and assurance here: "I give eternal life to them, and they shall never perish; and *no one shall snatch them out of My hand* " (John 10:28).

✓ *Purpose*...to put away any uncertainty in your heart and rejoice in the reality of life, eternal life! You don't need to *wish* for eternal life. Why? Because it is a reality if you are a Christian (1 John 5:13-14). The eternal God Himself, Jesus Christ, promised it—and that's a guarantee from the God who cannot lie.

✓ *Purpose*...to give your whole heart to God's use today... and all the days of your life! You don't want to *waste* your life. You have a stewardship. Your life is costly. It cost God the death of His Son. Use it daily. Use it wisely, willingly, and without withholding. Use it to bless others.

✓ *Purpose*...to share the good news of life in Christ with others. People the world over and throughout time have searched for the life that you now possess. Juan Ponce de León searched for the fountain of youth and never found it. False religions offer eternal life but cannot produce it. Only a personal relationship with Jesus Christ can give life—depth of life now and length of life for eternity. The fountain of life has been found! Share it with others! *Witness* to others about eternal life. Humanly speaking, their destiny depends on your faithfulness to share about your own life in Christ (Romans 10:9-10).

*Love is that condition
in which the happiness of another person
is essential to your own.*[17]

12

God's Powerful Promise of
Love

How often have you met a bona fide celebrity? Living in Southern California for almost 30 years, and working part of that time in Beverly Hills, gave me a few opportunities to at least recognize several movie stars. I never actually met any of them, but it was a thrill to go home and play "Guess who I saw today?" with my wife, Elizabeth.

But both Elizabeth and I did meet a music celebrity in person several years ago at a dinner given by some friends. Now, realize that, as I tell this story, this was a one-time event for us. We never expected to meet such a celebrity because we're not in those kinds of social circles. This musician was Hal David, the writer of the words for "What the World Needs Now Is Love." The music was composed by Burt Bacharach and sung by Jackie DeShannon.

Well, anyway, this songwriter was a very gracious and interesting man. It was fascinating to hear how he came to write the lyrics to this award-winning tune. And, as an added bonus that evening, the woman who sang the original release of this still-famous song was there with him. So, you guessed it! Our hosts asked these two "stars" to sing their well-known song! And before we realized what was happening, we—and everyone else in the entire restaurant—were all singing along with them. What a once-in-a-lifetime treat!

Discovering the Promise

If you know the hit tune I'm talking about, you are probably already humming along, right? And I'll bet you also agree with the message of the song. The world still needs love...of which there's still too little!

But note this powerful promise from God:

> *God has not given us a*
> *spirit of timidity,*
> *but of...love.*
> 2 Timothy 1:7

Love is a vital biblical quality to possess. But for both men and women, it is also an attitude that is often misunderstood. Our society confuses love with lust. Lust is a strong physical and/or sexual desire. It can occur without any associated feelings of love or affection, becoming a one-way street to self-fulfillment and self-gratification. As fallen creatures, our natural inclination is...

—∾— to take—not to give

—∾— to seek gratification—not to gratify

—∾— to seek understanding—not to understand

—∾— to be selfish—not to be selfless

God's kind of love, however, goes against all our human tendencies. Unlike lust and self-gratification, God's kind of love is directed outwardly toward others. That's why God's promise of love—His kind of love—is so important for us to understand. That's also why such love will revolutionize our lives. We must be careful not to confuse God's brand of love with what the world and our society would call love.

Understanding the Promise

This Bible promise—"God has not given us a spirit of timidity, but of...love"—was given to a young preacher named Timothy. He was facing some pretty stiff opposition. Paul, his mentor, wrote to encourage Timothy to refuse to be intimidated and fearful. He was to remember that God had already given him a powerful resource that would combat his fear—love.

1. *Love is possessed by all believers.*
Timothy is not the only person to whom God gave this powerful promise. God has given *every* believer the resource of His divine love, and that includes us. His love "has been poured out within our hearts through the Holy Spirit" (Romans 5:5).

This promise of His eternal, inexhaustible, and ever-present love should be most comforting. As a person, you have faced—and you will face—hardships, persecution, illness, and ultimately, death. But these adversities should not cause you to be fearful nor ruin the quality of your life. Why? Because nothing (including these afflictions) "shall be able to separate us from the love of God, which is in Christ Jesus our Lord" (Romans 8:39). Have no fear—God's love is near!

2. *Love is an act of your will.*

God desires that you freely give His love to others, beginning right at home to those nearest you. The Bible assumes that if you have received love from God, you will want to give love to others (1 John 4:19). Right? But like the other fruit of the Spirit (Galatians 5:22-23), loving others requires an act of your will. It's your choice. God's Word says you must choose to...

—∾— love your spouse (Colossians 3:19)

—∾— love your enemies (Luke 6:27)

—∾— love your neighbor (James 2:8)

—∾— love other believers (1 Peter 2:17)

—∾— love one another (1 John 3:11)

Examine your heart. Is the evidence of God's love there? Remember: "Every one who loves is born of God and knows God. The one who does not love does not know God, for God is love" (1 John 4:7-8).

3. *Love is serving God.*

Someone once asked Jesus which commandment in the Bible was the greatest. And Jesus' answer? "You shall love the Lord your God with all your heart, and with all your soul, and with all your mind, and with all your strength" (Mark 12:30).

What does it mean to love God with all your heart? It means we serve only one Master, God Himself (Matthew 6:24). Our devotion to our Lord will manifest itself in our service to Him. Just imagine the effect of such love-inspired service to God! It would truly turn the world upside down!

4. *Love is serving others.*

On that same occasion when Jesus gave the greatest commandment, He also added the second greatest: "You shall love your neighbor as yourself" (Mark 12:31). When we love God with all our hearts, God's love can't help but overflow into the lives of others. With all the love God has given us, we are to serve one another (Galatians 5:13).

Putting God's Power to Work

Did you know the depth of your spiritual life is actually measured by the depth of your love? If your first love is *yourself,* then your life will center on seeking your own pleasure, comfort, and welfare. Your focus will be on *your* personal goals, objectives, and successes. God and others then end up in the backseat behind your ambitions.

But, if you appropriate the God-given love that is promised to you, then your life will have an entirely different focus. It will center on pleasing God and seeking the welfare of others.

Don't forget: Love is a choice. And following these steps will help you make L-O-V-E's choices.

> L ook—Love is action. Look for opportunities to serve others. What can you do for someone else? Sit and listen? Lend a helping hand? Volunteer to take care of a need or problem?
>
> Does your neighbor need someone to watch his house while he is on vacation? Does someone in your church

need a ride on Sunday mornings? Open your eyes and your heart...and do something. Actively pursue love (1 Corinthians 14:1)!

O bey—Love is a fruit of the Spirit. If you are not walking with God in obedience, then God's love is not available through you to others. Keep the channel to God open with prayer and a pure life so that you can be an instrument of God's love to others.

V alue—Love is an incredibly powerful virtue to possess. Love should be your highest goal (1 Corinthians 13:13). Love is greater than faith and hope. Only a Christian can possess true love—God's love. It's a treasure money can't buy. It's a treasure the world can't produce. It's a treasure that is yours to value and a gift to share with others, starting with your family, and then extending to the family of God.

E njoy—Love of God and service to others should give you your greatest joy. Jesus loved you and me so much that He gave His life "for the joy set before Him" (Hebrews 12:2). Loving people should bring you life's highest joy!

Lord, make me an instrument of thy peace!
    Where there is hatred...let me sow love.
    Where there is injury...pardon.
    Where there is doubt...faith.
    Where there is despair...hope.
    Where there is darkness...light.
    Where there is sadness...joy.
                —SAINT FRANCIS OF ASSISI

13

God's Powerful Promise of
Peace

On several occasions I've come across this story I'm about to share. And, as a former army reservist, each time I hear or read about it, I have found the unusual set of events that occurred on a desolate island in the Philippines almost unbelievable. Today as I revisited the incredible details, I could only shake my head.

It seems that at the close of the Pacific Theater of World War II, every Japanese soldier surrendered...except four: Lieutenant Hiroo Onoda and three of his men. Somehow Lieutenant Onoda and his group never received their superior officer's message to surrender. Therefore, the holdouts would not believe the war was over!

For the next three decades, Onoda and his men sought to

avoid capture by the "enemy." In their minds, they were still at war. But slowly and surely, as the years passed by, one by one, the lieutenant's men were killed or surrendered...but not Onoda.

Can you imagine the shock this soldier's family must have felt when they were informed he was still alive? Onoda finally surrendered, 30 years after the war was over, on March 9, 1974, at age 53—but only after his former commander met him and personally read the orders that all combat activity was to cease. For Onoda, the war was over at last...30 years after the war ended!

Discovering the Promise

What about you...have you received the official communiqué yet? Has someone come to you and relayed the message?

"What message?" you say.

The message that the war is over!

"What war?" you ask.

The war between God and sinners.

What a great message! God is no longer at war with us. We "sinners" can have peace with God. (And pardon me, but I'm assuming that you consider yourself to be a sinner, too. Even the great apostle Paul confessed himself to be a sinner. In fact, he said, "I am the *worst*" of sinners—1 Timothy 1:15 NLT.)

But even though we are all sinners, God has made peace with us through His Son, the Lord Jesus Christ (Romans 5:1). The war is over. And because we are at peace *with* God, we can now enter into Jesus' powerful promise of the peace *of* God:

> *Peace I leave with you;*
> *My peace I give you.*
> JOHN 14:27

Understanding the Promise

Peace! A heart at rest. Serenity. This is what the whole world is looking for, isn't it? Now, the *worldly* kind of peace is defined as peace without conflict—world peace. But the peace *of God* is vastly different. The peace of God is tranquility...in any, all, and every circumstance. And it's something God extends to you.

How can you enjoy this kind of peace? Read on!

1. *God's peace is available.*

Again, the world is desperately searching for peace—peace without conflict. People are looking for tranquility in religion (with or without the meditation!), in solitude (isolated camps and retreat centers), and in countless other ways (medication, burning candles, playing music for relaxation, and so forth).

But as a child of God, you don't have to go looking for peace. You already have God's powerful promise of peace. You already possess the "secret" to confident assurance...no matter what. Jesus offers you this kind of peace—His peace. He says, "Peace I leave with you; My peace I give you." Yes, Jesus is offering you His peace—the peace of God. But unless you accept the offer and apply it or use it, it won't do you any good. For instance...

Let's say someone gave you a million dollars. You then hid the money under your mattress or in the cookie jar in the kitchen, and left it there. Would that money do you any good? Would it better your life? Would it feed you or your family? Pay your bills? Help others? Of course not! You have to *use* the money for it to do any good. And the same is true of God's promise of peace—you have to use it. It's there, but you must apply it to your life.

2. *God's peace comes with trust.*

Amazingly, the Bible says we are "not to be anxious about anything." What are we to do instead? "By prayer and petition, with thanksgiving, present your requests to God" (Philippians 4:6 NIV). In other words, you are to *trust* God with your circumstances, with your "anything" and your "everything," even your "nothing"!

And the result? "The peace of God, which transcends all understanding, will guard your hearts and your minds in Christ Jesus" (verse 7). That's God's promise. But you can choose not to trust God. You can choose to continue to be anxious and worried. It's your choice. And, believe me, your choice will make a difference in your interaction with others and the way you view your circumstances!

Jesus' 12 disciples, in spite of how close they were to Jesus, the Prince of Peace, had to *learn* that peace comes from trust (Luke 8:22-25). Here's the scene: A fierce storm was raging on the Sea of Galilee. The disciples were desperately rowing their boat, trying to get to shore. While they toiled, Jesus was fast asleep in the boat. In panic, they woke Jesus up and shouted over the howling wind, "Master, Master, we're going to drown!"

As the waves crashed over the sides and into the boat, Jesus calmly rebuked the wind and the violent waters. Then He asked His men, "Where is your faith?" (verses 24-25). In other words, "Where is your trust in God's ability to protect and care for you?"

Dear friend, God is asking you (and me!) the same question. "Where is your faith? Where is your trust?" If you are anxious about anything—a job or the lack of one, your children or the lack of them, your future, your health (well, you know the list of "the cares of this world"!), then give those unsettling issues over to God. Trust in His ability to help. Then enjoy and experience God's promise of calming peace. Oh, what a difference *that* will make!

3. *God's peace comes with obedience.*

Even though Elizabeth and I are not even approaching the grave (at least we think!), Psalm 23 ("The Lord is my shepherd...") is a favorite for each of us. In fact, we've written two books about this psalm that ministers peace to all.[18] It conjures up a mental picture of sheep lounging at rest on green rolling hills, basking in the presence and protection of their good shepherd. This peaceful, pastoral psalm was written by David, the king of Israel, who was a shepherd himself. It is a perfect picture of God's perfect peace.

Now, contrast this psalm and its peaceful scenario with this troubled psalm written by David some years later: "My body wasted away through my groaning all day long....My vitality was drained away as with the fever heat of summer" (Psalm 32:3-4).

"David," we ask, "what happened to your peace?"

David then confesses, "I kept silent about my sin" (verse 3).

"Well, how did you deal with this turmoil, David? How did you recapture God's peace in your heart?"

David then explains, "I acknowledged my sin to [God], and my iniquity I did not hide. I said, 'I will confess my transgressions to the LORD'" (verse 5).

Now note how David's "tune" changed as a result of being obedient to Scripture and confessing his sin: "Be *glad* in the Lord and *rejoice,* you righteous ones, and shout for *joy,* all you upright in heart!" (verse 11).

Can't you sense the joy and peace that returned to David's soul? And aren't you thankful that this same sense of peace is available to you when you seek to remember God's powerful promise of peace?

Putting God's Power to Work

It's a fact: You *have* peace with God through Jesus Christ. The war is over! Christ's death on your behalf is a settled reality. This should calm any and all of the stormy waters you must navigate...daily and forever.

But now comes the challenge of living out the peace of God *in* your life. Peace in your heart equals peace in your home. Jesus promised to leave His peace with you, and He did. So agree to take Christ at His word. Apply His powerful promise of peace to your life-situation daily.

What challenges are causing you the most concern? What problems are robbing you of one of God's greatest gifts to you—His peace?

I will address this more in the upcoming study section. But for now...

✓ *Remember*—God has promised you peace, period! It's yours for the taking. So it's your choice. Do you want to continue fretting and worrying yourself sick? Or do you want a change? Do you want to allow God's peace to invade your heart?

✓ *Respond*—Sit down and consider the pattern of your reactions to your recent circumstances. Is it one of peace, or panic?

If you find yourself stressed or anxious, then change things. Stop worrying and experience God's peace by praying to Him. Place your worries and fears into His mighty and capable hands. Ask Him to strengthen your faith in His ability to help you through your problems. Ask Him to obliterate any anger you might have. Ask Him for His help in turning things around so that you honor and glorify Him by exhibiting His peace in every situation. Ask Him now!

*The greatest unused power
in the world
is the Holy Spirit of
the living God.*[19]

14

God's Powerful Promise of
Power

A s I read my Bible, I love to follow the lives of specific men and women and watch how God transforms and uses them. One of my favorites is Stephen. We first meet him when he is selected by the early church apostles to take care of the needs of the widows in Jerusalem (Acts 6:1-6). A little later we see him performing "great wonders and signs among the people" (verse 8), and then we see him standing before the rulers of Israel and powerfully admonishing them for their unbelief in Christ (Acts 7:2-53). Where did this transforming power come from? How was Stephen changed from a server of widows into such a bold spokesman for God?

We see another dynamic transformation in the inspiring story of Aquila and Priscilla. We first meet this married couple in

121

Corinth, where they make tents for a living (Acts 18:1-3). From that point on, their lives explode into an incredible display of powerful ministry.[20]

— opened their home to the formation of churches in two different cities,

— invited missionaries, including the apostle Paul, to stay with them in their home,

— worked shoulder to shoulder in service and ministry, and

— forged ahead in fearless service to God and His people, even in the face of persecution.

Yes, it's true—their powerful service to several early churches brought great persecution and danger upon them. Paul wrote this about these two fearless people in his letter to the church in Rome (which, by the way, met in this couple's house!): "Greet Priscilla and Aquila, my fellow workers in Christ Jesus. They risked their lives for me. Not only I but all the churches of the Gentiles are grateful to them" (Romans 16:3-4 NIV).

Where did this dynamic couple and fearless Stephen get their power for ministry? Let's read on to find out their secret.

Discovering the Promise

Backtrack for a minute with me about 30 years, to the beginnings of the Christian movement in ancient Israel. Jesus Christ had risen from the dead and was about to return to the right hand of the Father. But before He left earth, He commissioned His followers to "make disciples of all nations" (Matthew 28:19). How would these untrained and uneducated people carry out this worldwide ministry?

They, along with all the disciples who would follow—including you!—would be "empowered" for ministry. Here's Christ's promise:

> *You shall receive power*
> *when the Holy Spirit has*
> *come upon you.*
> ACTS 1:8

And friend, as with the disciples—and as with other powerful servants God has used—God never asks us to attempt *anything* for Him that He doesn't provide *all* the resources we need to be successful.

Understanding the Promise

As we begin to look at this promise of power, we must understand that Jesus didn't promise His disciples—or you or me—*worldly positions* of power and authority. That's what people in the world are looking for—positions of power by which they can rule over others. But Jesus' promise to His followers then, and to you and me today, is power for *spiritual purposes*. Such power has unique qualities about it.

1. *God's power comes from the Holy Spirit.*

The power that the world promotes is power generated from personal strength or beauty, superior intellect, or shrewd manipulation. But the power Jesus offered to His disciples—and promises to us, too—is power from the indwelling ministry of the Holy Spirit—"when the Holy Spirit has come upon you."

In the Old Testament, the Holy Spirit empowered a small number of specific individuals, such as Moses, David, and others, for specific purposes. But from the New Testament onward, the

Holy Spirit has come into the life of *every* follower of Christ—and is in us to stay. That means you have His empowerment available for a lifetime—for a ministry, for a God-honoring life, at all times!

2. God's power comes at salvation.

The disciples received their power on the Day of Pentecost, when "they were all filled with the Holy Spirit" (Acts 2:4). You received that same power when you put your faith and trust in Jesus Christ (2 Corinthians 1:21-22). So you don't need to ask for power or more power. At salvation, you received all the power you will ever need. You only need to tap into it by walking in obedience, by walking by the Spirit (Galatians 5:16).

3. God's power is to be used for witnessing.

Jesus promised the disciples would receive power for a specific task. He said, "You shall receive power...and you shall be my witnesses." After the coming of the Holy Spirit, Jesus' followers were empowered to tell others what they had seen and heard while they were with Jesus.

We, too, are empowered to be Jesus' witnesses. We, too, are to tell others what we have seen, heard, and learned through God's Word concerning Jesus Christ, and what we have experienced in our relationship with Him. What does this power for witnessing and ministry enable us to do? It gives us...

— conviction to speak out for Christ,

— courage to speak up for Christ,

— confidence to speak about Christ, and

— capacity to speak for Christ.

4. *God's power is perfected in weakness.*

Another favorite verse I love and draw upon (every day!) is 2 Corinthians 12:9: "My grace is sufficient for you, for power is perfected in weakness." Do you want God's power in your life and for your battles? If so, stop trying to do things in your own strength. Give up your puny human efforts. Instead, turn to God for His end-all strength. Exchange your weaknesses for His power.

5. *God's power is for service.*

Where, we wonder, did Stephen and Aquila and Priscilla get the amazing power their lives and ministries required? Answer: From the Holy Spirit. Christians are empowered with "spiritual gifts"—divine enablements that are to be used "for the common good" (1 Corinthians 12:7). This supernatural giftedness allows us to serve God and His people with sustained power. On our own, we're weak and inadequate. But with God's empowerment, we can have an incredible impact, whether it's talking to a hostile crowd as Stephen did, or the energetic and far-reaching ministry of helps and service demonstrated in the lives of Aquila and Priscilla.

Putting God's Power to Work

✓ *Realize*…the importance of living a Spirit-filled life. The Holy Spirit empowers obedient believers. So stay on top of things in your life. Guard against sin, and watch your communication and your actions. And when you slip up, be quick to make matters right with God (confess your sin) and with others (ask for forgiveness)!

✓ *Rely*...on the indwelling power of the Holy Spirit in your life. He will never leave you. And His power is fully available to you anytime...and for all times...and for all situations. When life gets tough...or sticky...or begins to fall apart, ask God for His help. Rely on His power in your times of trial.

✓ *Remember*...why God's power was given to you. You are to be a witness of Him. Concentrate on being an example of what God can do in a life. That will speak volumes and perhaps open up an opportunity for you to share what *you* have seen, heard, and learned about Jesus Christ. Don't worry. God will enable you with His wisdom, lead you into His perfect timing, and give you His power to live in your situation.

✓ *Relax*...in knowing that God has given you His power for ministry. Whatever that ministry is, He will enable you to serve Him and His people. What a blessing you will be to others! So relax! The less you try to use your own abilities, the more there will be of God's power and His limitless abilities.

✓ *Respond*...to God's call to serve. The church, the body of Christ, needs each of us serving one another. Pray about how you can respond to God's call.

If there be a God,
the learned ones say
He is billions and billions
of light years away.

I'm not a scientist,
but one thing I know,
The Lord is with me
wherever I go.[21]

15

God's Powerful Promise of
Presence

I was an only child, and this had some great benefits for me. I didn't have to share my toys with any brothers or sisters. I also didn't have to share my parents' affection with other siblings. I was pretty much the center of attention. But there was one daily problem. I didn't have anyone to play with! So I was always trying to make friends and find playmates.

Very few people in this world like to be alone. And that's biblical! God created us, both male and female, to be social beings. God knew from the beginning of time that man needed companionship. It was God who noticed and said, "It is not good for the man to be alone; I will make him a helper suitable for him" (Genesis 2:18). And *voila*—it was done! God created Eve, gave her to Adam, and the two became the first married couple. Now they had each other.

Even if you are not married, you probably have some friends who are good companions. Also, as a member of a church, you have the body, other church members, to come alongside you in good times as well as in times of difficulty. But when God said, "It is not good for the man to be alone," He may have been commenting on more than just marriage relationships and more than relationships with friends. He was also speaking to the spiritual realm.

Discovering God's Promise

What God wants to do for you, as stated in this next promise, is repeated over and over throughout the Bible. Regardless of whether you have any other person around you, you will still have Him—His presence—with you...at all times, no matter what is happening, where you are, or what you are facing. One of these powerful promises of God's presence was given to Joshua, His servant:

> *Do not tremble or be dismayed,*
> *for the LORD your God is with you*
> *wherever you go.*
> JOSHUA 1:9

We've already met Joshua in this book, and we'll be exposed to this wonderful man again. But for now, remember that he was Israel's leader for the conquest of the Promised Land. Joshua was guaranteed success in the overthrow of the heathen people if he did certain things, such as obey God and heed His Word as revealed in the book of the law (verse 8).

But God had more encouragement for Joshua. God gave Joshua the powerful promise above. God promised that *He* would be with Joshua throughout the whole campaign of winning the land—and then some! In other words, God would be with Joshua his whole life.

What a promise! It didn't matter what would happen, or who would be with Joshua, or even if he had to stand alone. Why? Because God would be there.

Understanding God's Promise

Now, you might be reading along and thinking, *But that's the Old Testament. God said that He would be with Joshua, but does this promise apply to me as well?*

1. *God's presence is for you.*

Yes, dear friend! God's promise of His presence applies to you as well. How can we know this? Well, the primary reason is that Jesus said the same thing to His New Testament followers: "And lo, I am with you always, even to the end of the age" (Matthew 28:20). Jesus' promise was made to His disciples, but we know we are included in this promise because He added, "...to the end of the age."

That's the promise that we Christians can claim—God will be with us for as long as we live. None of us can make such a statement about another person. People who are near to us will die and leave, but God will always be present with us...even through such a hard time and its aftermath. What a powerful and comforting promise!

2. *God's presence is real.*

Perhaps in a pensive mood, the psalmist asked the question, "Where can I go from Your Spirit? Or where can I flee from Your presence?" (Psalm 139:7). The writer then listed all the places he might go…but not without God's knowledge and presence! He named places like the height of the sky, the depths of the sea, the farthest ends of the earth, even into complete darkness. And yet, the poet finally acknowledged that God would be there in those unreachable places with him. He ultimately had to conclude and recognize the presence of God wherever he went.

The truth of God's presence especially brought Elizabeth, my wife, great comfort twice when we were apart from one another. One time was when Elizabeth's scheduled flight home was suddenly rerouted due to a blizzard. There wasn't any way she could let me know what had happened. She remembers sitting on that plane praying, "God, not one person in this world knows where I am." Then she remembered God's presence and added, "But You do!" His presence reassured her when she was "lost in space" and alone…or so she initially and erroneously thought!

The other time was when Elizabeth underwent major surgery. She was wheeled into a preparation room, and I joined her. There I prayed for and with her. I was present for all the preliminaries, until finally the time came when she had to be rolled off to the surgery suite…and I wasn't allowed to go with her.

All she could do was lie there, helpless and praying, "Lord, yea, though I may be walking through the valley of the shadow of death (I don't know what the surgeon may find!), and yea, though I am entering the unknown (she had never had surgery before!), and yea, though I'm being put under with anesthetics (and may never wake up to see Jim again!), Thou art with me!"

And do you know what? God was…and He is! When you cannot be with someone in a time of need, God can…and is!

3. *God's presence is a good thing.*

King David was described by God as "a man after My own

heart" (Acts 13:22). Obviously David had many sterling qualities. One of those was his passion to be in God's presence. Hear how he expresses his desire:

> One thing I have asked from the LORD, that I shall seek; that I may dwell in the house of the LORD all the days of my life, to behold the beauty of the LORD, and to meditate in His temple (Psalm 27:4).

Sadly, this is not the primary passion of many Christians. Rather than spending their time seeking God and desiring to live in His presence moment by moment, they are like Adam and Eve. (I'm quite sure you know the story!) Adam and Eve at one time walked with God in the cool of the day, but when they sinned, they "hid themselves from the presence of the LORD God among the trees of the garden" (Genesis 3:8). Their sin altered the relationship they had enjoyed with God.

And sin can do the same to us. If you sense that your relationship with God is a little distant, confess it to God. Do your part to close the gap, and again revel in the truth of God's presence in your life.

4. *God's presence is a comfort.*

If you are like me (and probably everyone else!), you often wish that you could avoid pain, grief, loss, sorrow, failure, and a host of other difficulties. You even wish you could rid your life of those small daily frustrations that constantly wear you down. But hear how God comes to your aid in times of trouble:

> The righteous cry and the LORD hears, and delivers them out of all their troubles. The LORD is near to the brokenhearted, and saves those who are crushed in spirit. Many are the afflictions of the righteous; but

the LORD delivers him out of them all (Psalm 34:17-
19).

Did you catch all that? God promises to be a source of power,
courage, and strength and to help you through your problems.
Sometimes He chooses to deliver you from your problems. At
other times, He gives you the strength to endure through them.
Either way, His presence is with you!

So, when difficulties strike (and strike they will!), don't get
upset and frustrated with God. Instead, thank Him that He is
present with you. Acknowledge that you need Him at your side
to help in times of trouble. Cry out to Him! Run to Him! Cling
to Him! Count on His presence. No matter how bad it gets, the
Lord is with you. He is always with His children.

Putting God's Power to Work

Joshua is one person, and the psalmist is another. But how
about *you?* Have you thought much about God's constant and
abiding presence with *you,* in *your* home, in *your* difficulties?
When you do, it will make a difference in your life and in your
faith in God. How?

The fact of God's presence should take root in your life. You
should talk about God when you are with other believers. You
should make it a point to insert His name into your conversa-
tions. You should refer to Him often...with every breath!

Here's how I practice the presence of God. When I receive
a paycheck, before I open it, I pray. When I receive a letter or
get off the phone from talking to someone with a problem, I
pray. When I get in the car or on an airplane, I pray. When I eat,
I pray. When I'm sad, I pray...glad, I pray...fearful, I pray...in
need, I pray.

Yes, this may appear to be about prayer, but why do I pray? Because I believe God is present with me, hearing me talk and pray. And because I am constantly fine-tuning my awareness of God's presence, I tend to automatically include Him in everything. You see, it isn't just me: It is the two of us!

> Christ is the head of [my] house,
> the unseen guest at every meal,
> the silent listener to every conversation.[22]

As the little rhyme at the beginning of this chapter affirms (and with the pronouns changed), "but one thing I know, the Lord is with me wherever I go." And I would add, "and whatever I go *through!*"

He clothes the lilies, feeds the birds;
Would He to you, then, pay less heed?
Look up to Him with prayerful heart,
He will supply your every need.[23]

16

God's Powerful Promise of
Provision

A s a pastor for several decades, I have spent countless hours counseling and encouraging men and single mothers as they endeavor to support their families. I can tell you that many of them suffered from ulcers, high blood pressure, heart problems, and a number of other illnesses due to the weight of the burden to provide financially for their families. The rigors of the demands on their jobs and their constant state of worry and anxiety take a daily toll on providers' health and well-being. God's curse on Adam has definitely become a harsh reality in their lives. As God told Adam, "By the sweat of your face you shall eat bread" (Genesis 3:19).

But there's good news! There is one kind of provision you as a Christian never have to worry about, and that is God's provision for you.

Discovering the Promise

Hidden in the writings of the apostle Paul is a powerful promise that sustained him every day of his life. And dear friend, it can sustain you, too! Here's the scene...

Paul is in jail (again!) for his faith. Heavy on his heart is his concern for his good friends in faraway Philippi. So Paul takes "pen" in hand and writes to his friends in Christ. In his letter he thanks these folks for a gift of financial support they had sent to him (Philippians 4:18). Then Paul, the master writer, uses the Philippians' provision for his needs as an illustration of how God will provide for their needs. For, you see, they were not a wealthy people—they gave to Paul out of "their extreme poverty" (2 Corinthians 8:2 NIV). What did Paul say to encourage these needy people?

> *My God shall supply all your needs*
> *according to His riches in glory*
> *in Christ Jesus.*
> PHILIPPIANS 4:19

Paul gave these poor Christians a promise of God's provision. And friend, the hope he passed on to his comrades extends its way across the centuries all the way to you and me.

Why, we might wonder, could Paul be so confident in his promise? Because Paul understood the promise and the Promise Giver.

Understanding the Promise

1. *A personal provider.*

Paul had a personal relationship with his provider, whom he

referred to as "my God." By the time he wrote this letter, Paul had walked with God for more than 20 years. His continual trust in God to provide for his every need had resulted in a close relationship with his heavenly Father. Paul knew God. Therefore, he was confident that God would provide for His children.

Our first order of business is to ask an important question: Are you a child of God? God's promise of provision applies only to His children. Can you speak of God as "my God"? Now would be the perfect time to assess your relationship with God through Jesus Christ.

Have you accepted Christ's payment for your sin? Have you received Jesus Christ as your Lord and Savior? Look again at the chapter entitled "God's Powerful Promise of...Life" and the prayer on page 101. Becoming a Christian is the ultimate first step in putting God's promises to work in your life.

2. *A physical provision.*

And what does God want to do for you? Notice the promise: "My God shall supply *all your needs.*" Not your *wants*, but your *needs*. In other words, you can always count on God to supply all that is required to sustain your physical life.

And what are your needs? Jesus said that your heavenly Father knows what your needs are: What you need to *eat*...what you need to *drink*...what you need for *clothing* (Matthew 6:31-32). Pretty basic, isn't it? Friend, there is no physical need God is not able to meet. You can trust God to meet "all your needs."

3. *A plentiful provision.*

It's impossible for us to comprehend God's "riches in glory"! They are boundless, limitless, infinite! And it was out of God's abundant storehouse that the Philippians' needs would be met.

And it is out of God's plentiful riches in glory that He provides for your needs, too.

And here's the backbone of this splendid promise: God provides *according to* His riches, not *out of* His riches. Do you see the difference? If God's supply was merely *out of His riches*, there would be a limit on His provision. His supply would have to be doled out, little by little. But no, our great, unlimited God takes care of us *according to His riches*—riches that are limitless. That means its provision for us is limitless...and so is God's promise.

I know this is hard to grasp because we are grappling with the nature of an infinite God! But trust God's Word—there is enough of God's provision to meet any need you will ever have in your whole lifetime. As the saying goes, Place your needs up against His riches, and they will soon disappear.

4. *A privileged position.*

Such plentiful provision from God could only happen because of our relationship with Christ, because we are "in Christ Jesus." Jesus makes it possible for us to have access to God so we can "come boldly to the throne of grace, that we may obtain mercy and find grace to help in time of need" (Hebrews 4:16 NKJV). Again, do you have that privileged relationship with God through Jesus Christ? Jesus said, "I am the way, and the truth, and the life; no one comes to the Father, but through Me" (John 14:6).

Isn't God a great God? He will provide for our needs. What a magnificent promise! So whatever your need is today, whether it's financial, physical, emotional, or spiritual, boldly take that need to God. Then watch as He supplies "all your needs according to His riches in glory in Christ Jesus."

With God's example of provision fresh in your mind, take a few minutes and put God's promise to work in your life.

Putting God's Power to Work

✓ *Take time*...to thank God for His provision thus far in your life. In Him you have an abundance! God has truly fulfilled His promise, and your needs have been adequately cared for. And probably even a number of your "wants" have been supplied as well! You can certainly say, "Thank You!"

✓ *Take a moment*...to reflect on your responsibilities. You are a steward of all that you possess. A steward is one who takes care of the goods of another. And, in your case, God is that "another." You'll notice I didn't say you *own* these items. All that you have—your home, your car, your children, your everything!—is *entrusted* to you by God and is an opportunity for stewardship.

✓ *Take action*...on what you now understand about God's provision and your stewardship of His property. What can you do to be a wise steward, a better steward?

—Be content with what God has provided (1 Timothy 6:6-8).

—Give back to God a portion of what He has given to you (1 Corinthians 16:2).

—Have a budget to account for what God has provided.

—Make a list of ways to cut expenses.

—Learn to wait and pray over major purchases.

—Declare a "day of fasting" from spending money.

—Remember...

God is able to make all grace abound to you,
that always having all sufficiency
in everything, you may have an
abundance for every good deed.
2 CORINTHIANS 9:8

The purpose of your life is far greater
than your own personal fulfillment,
your peace of mind, or even your happiness.
It's far greater than your family, your career,
or even your wildest dreams and ambitions.
If you want to know why you were placed
on this planet,
you must begin with God.
You were born by his purpose
and for his purpose.
—RICK WARREN

17

God's Powerful Promise of Purpose

I'm sure you have heard stories of people who have survived incredible difficulties. Maybe you've even heard about those who have lived through the deprivations and inhumane treatment endured as prisoners of war. You may have read about the life of Corrie ten Boom and her prison-camp years. Her story became very vivid to me and my family, as we toured Dachau, the infamous World War II concentration camp in Germany. One man's real-life "survivor" story of one of these camps is especially revealing and at the same time enlightening and educational.

Victor Frankl was an Austrian psychiatrist who spent years in a German concentration camp. Life in the camp was incredibly harsh and brutal. The prisoners were forced to work long hours, with little food, insufficient clothing, and inadequate shelter. As time dragged on, Frankl noticed that some of the prisoners collapsed under the pressure, gave up, and died, while others continued to stay alive under the same demands.

What made the difference? Using his psychiatric training, Dr. Frankl talked to the other inmates in the evenings. Over the months he noticed a pattern. Those prisoners who had something to live for, an objective that gave a sense of meaning to their lives or a purpose, were the ones who seemed to be able to mobilize their strength and survive.

As Frankl continued to interview his fellow prisoners, he found out that their objectives for living were individual and different. Each survivor had a focus and a passion that kept him alive. And Frankl was no exception. He had begun a book and had a fierce desire to survive and finish it. After the war, Victor Frankl completed what had motivated him to stay alive—his book!

Discovering the Promise

Frankl's experience illustrates for us the power of purpose. There is nothing as potent as a life lived with passion and purpose. The survivors in Frankl's concentration camp focused on a purpose that was personally inspired. In Frankl's case it was his book. Another man had a girlfriend he hoped to marry as soon as the war was over.

But what if you could have a purpose that wasn't inspired by your own desires? A purpose that came from a higher source— a divine source—from God? Wouldn't that be a grand purpose indeed? This brings us to yet another of the promises of what God wants to do for you:

> *Before I formed you in the womb I knew you*
> *and before you were born I consecrated you;*
> *I have appointed you....*
> JEREMIAH 1:5

God promised Jeremiah that he had a God-given purpose. God had *appointed* Jeremiah as a prophet to the nations. Obviously that's not God's purpose for you or me today. But just as God promised Jeremiah a purpose, so He promises us a purpose. Do you know what God's promised purpose is for your life? I hope you do. I am sure you can see that having a purpose for your life, and especially God's purpose, has great significance.

Understanding the Promise

Here's a little background information for you about Jeremiah's day. The sixth century BC was a chaotic time politically, morally, and spiritually for God's people in the tiny country of Judah. Babylon, Egypt, and Assyria were battling for world supremacy, and Judah was caught in the middle. In the midst of this chaos, God called Jeremiah to be His prophet.

Of course God knew Jeremiah would object and try to decline the offer. So God preempted Jeremiah's objection with a powerful promise. God's promise was based on His sovereign power and His divine purpose. God's voice boomed out of heaven, "Before...you were born I consecrated you; I have appointed you a prophet to the nations."

What effect did God's promise have on the reluctant Jeremiah? Knowing that God had set him apart for a special assignment became Jeremiah's assurance in the years to come when he was persecuted and ridiculed because of his mission.

And friend, God's promise of purpose can serve as an anchor and assurance for you as well. How? And what are some benefits of God's promise of purpose for your life—benefits that will bless you?

1. *God's purpose gives meaning to your life.*

Life makes little or no sense without an understanding that all roads lead back to God and His purposes (Romans 8:28). Without God, your life has no meaning, and you have no hope (Ephesians 2:12). Like Jeremiah, your existence takes on meaning when you know and understand your purpose. Jeremiah's purpose was determined by God and for God...and so is yours. The prophet's life took on a special significance, a boldness and courage, because he knew exactly what his purpose was. And the same can be true of you. For meaning in life, look to your purpose.

2. *God's purpose is unique for you.*

Has it registered yet? *You* are special to God! And for that reason, God has sovereignly prepared you for a purpose, for your own unique contribution. Jeremiah was uniquely prepared for the task he was asked to accomplish, and so are you. You have been given a unique set of spiritual gifts (1 Corinthians 12:4-11), a unique personality, and unique life experiences, all to be used in a unique way by God. Realizing that God has a specific purpose for you should keep you from ever feeling discouraged or inadequate.

It's a good practice to pray daily and ask, What can I do for others today...and everyday...to encourage them toward their unique purpose? And go ahead—ask those people how you can pray specifically for them.

3. *God's purpose requires patience.*

Now, back to Jeremiah. No one knows how old Jeremiah was when he received this promise from God. Some theologians speculate he was between 20 to 30 years old. If that's true, then Jeremiah lived almost half of his life in a tiny village without knowing about the grand purpose God had for him.

That's a long time! But like Jeremiah, you must patiently wait for God to reveal and unfold His purpose for your life. And like Jeremiah, you must be faithful right where you are, right now, today! While you wait patiently on the Lord, you must do what you already know to be God's will for your life. Which brings us to our next point...

4. *God's purpose requires obedience.*

Discovering and fulfilling God's ongoing purpose for your life begins with obediently following His revealed purpose for your life *today*. That's what prepared Jeremiah for use by God. If you read the book of the Bible that bears his name, you'll discover that very few, if any, people desired to serve God in any way in Jeremiah's day. Yet God could—and did—use Jeremiah because he had not disqualified himself through disobedience. He was qualified to serve God because of his faithful, daily obedience.

Remember...God's purpose for your life is realized and unfolded with your every act of obedience. Obedience *is* God's purpose today for you. This is God's starting point for you. Then stand back and behold!...as God reveals the next step in your future and His purpose for your life.

Putting God's Power to Work

Are you excited yet? God promises that He has a purpose for you. That should add a dash of excitement to your life! But...are you wondering, *What is my purpose?*

Let me encourage you here. Like Jeremiah's, your purpose will have a unique nature to it. But God's purpose also has a thread that is common for all His people. Here's how you can put God's promise of purpose to work in your life today and every single day. Test yourself...and think it over!

✓ God's purpose is that you come to repentance (2 Peter 3:9). Have you?

✓ God's purpose is that you be conformed to the image of His Son (Romans 8:29). Are you in process? Do changes need to occur?

✓ God's purpose, if you are married, is that you as a husband love your wife, and that you as a wife love and respect your husband (Ephesians 5:22-33). How do you rate?

✓ God's purpose, if you have children, is that you care for and train them spiritually (Ephesians 6:4). How can you do a better job in the Parenting Department?

✓ God's purpose is that you keep yourself pure (1 Thessalonians 4:4). How can you pursue this?

✓ God's purpose is that you be His witness (Acts 1:8). Is this happening? If not, why not?

✓ God's purposes fulfilled *today* will guide you into God's purposes for your *tomorrow*. Just be faithful. Are you?

> *Man, made in the image of God, has a*
> *purpose—to be in relationship to God,*
> *who is there. Man forgets his purpose*
> *and thus he forgets who he is*
> *and what life means.*[25]
>
> FRANCIS A. SCHAEFFER

O God of peace, control my life,
No longer will I flee,
For I shall never know soul-rest
Until I rest in Thee.[26]

18

God's Powerful Promise of
Rest

For almost 30 years my family and I lived in the Los Angeles area. We loved it! And there's no doubt about it—Los Angeles is a city that never sleeps. It doesn't matter what time you are out and about. The roads, the streets, and the freeways are always packed with cars and people. But busyness and a hectic schedule is not unique to Los Angeles. My New York son-in-law, Paul, leaves the house before daylight to catch a train into Manhattan, and returns on that same train after dark. This dark-to-dark scenario is repeated for many people in almost every city around the world.

Whether we like it or not, or choose it or not, we are all members—or becoming members—of the "Busyness Club." As the pace of the world continues to pick up with faster travel, faster Internet access, faster computers (and don't forget fast food!), men, women, and even children(!) are finding less and less time to rest.

Discovering the Promise

We all know the pressure of working in order to provide for our needs. Plus, many of us must take the time to maintain a loving and caring relationship with our families. For a Christian, there is the added stewardship of serving in some capacity at one's church. Fulfilling all these duties and obligations takes time—time that must somehow be coordinated in the midst of what is a jam-packed life.

How can we find help for dealing with the hectic pace of life? This next powerful promise provides the answer:

> *Come to Me,*
> *all who are weary and heavy-laden,*
> *and I will give you rest.*
> Matthew 11:28

Understanding the Promise

I love this verse, and I imagine that you do, too. Just reading it causes me to exhale (whew!) and enjoy a measure of rest. What was it that moved Jesus to make this reassuring statement?

A quick answer is that the religious leaders of Jesus' day placed so many rules on the people that their "religion" had caused them to be "weary and heavy-laden." The people were weary from all of the rules and regulations that were impossible to fulfill. In short, they were worn out. Pleasing God seemed hopeless.

Enter Jesus! In this powerful promise, Jesus invited His audience—and us, too—to "Come to Me...and I will give you rest."

His summons was to *come* participate in the promise of *rest...* which only He can *give*.

Now the question is, What does this promise of rest mean?

1. *Rest is part of God's plan.*

God's rest is a common theme throughout the Bible. For instance...

— *God rested* on the seventh day to mark the completion of creation.

— *God's people rested* on the seventh day to rest, to refresh their souls, and to worship Him.

— *God's earth rested* as a result of God's command that the people allow the soil to rest every seven years (Leviticus 25:4).

This was God's plan—rest for worship, rest for His people, and rest for His earth. (Sounds good, doesn't it?) Obviously, rest is supremely important to God. Therefore, it should be important to us to ensure that we rest our bodies, refresh our souls, and worship God. Remember, rest is part of God's plan.

But there's more! Read on.

2. *Rest is a gift of God.*

Rest is a gift all good parents give to their children. In fact, neglect is defined by the U.S. court system as "the deliberate failure to meet the physical needs of a child," rest being one of those needs.[27] Now can you imagine Jesus' heartache when He saw His "children" so abused and neglected by an improper and incomplete understanding of the rest that was rightfully theirs?

In contrast to the religious leaders, Jesus offered mankind God's original design for rest to "all who are weary and heavy-laden." His rest included perfect fellowship and harmony with God. But there was one condition—God's offer of rest could become a reality only if and when the people heeded Jesus' invitation to "come to Me."

And dear friend, Jesus' offer of the gift of rest and refreshment is extended to you and to me as well. God promises spiritual rest. His rest provides freedom from guilt over sin, deliverance from fear and despair, continued guidance and help from the Holy Spirit, and ultimate eternal rest.

There is no reason for you to continue to be "weary and heavy-laden" when you heed Christ's call to "come to Me." In Christ you will find relief and refreshment in a new relationship with God. Remember, rest is a gift of God.

3. Rest is important for a balanced life.

Rest and refreshment in Christ...doesn't that sound great and inviting? I am praying that you are enjoying a spiritual relationship with Jesus Christ. This is the ultimate rest that everyone longs for!

But what about the physical realm? Often (for some of us, that's every minute we're awake!) our bodies tell us when it's time to take a rest. We feel tired, weary, exhausted.

Jesus revealed He understood all about our need for physical rest and all about our busy lives when He arranged for His disciples to get away from the crowds in a boat. His men were so busy they didn't even have time to eat (Mark 6:31-32). (Does this describe your schedule? It sure describes mine, especially as I am working against clocks in four different time zones!)

The disciples needed physical rest for what was to come. And surely you have this need, too! We so need the rest that refreshes us from what has gone before and prepares us for what is to come. (And, for your information, the next event on the disciples' hectic schedule was the feeding of the 5,000!—Mark 6:33-44.)

How are you doing in the Rest Department? Are there signs that you are not getting enough physical relaxation? Signs such as grumpiness, irritability, a short fuse? God has important work for you to do in His service. So do your part by getting some rest. Remember, rest is important for a balanced life.

Putting God's Power to Work

To review, God has promised us heaven's rest in the future. How wonderful that we can look forward to that eternal rest! Such a promise keeps us going for a long time, doesn't it? But we can also experience God's rest in the here and now, both spiritually and physically. Ask yourself these questions to make sure you are fully experiencing God's promise of rest, both now and ultimately in the future.

✓ Have you come to the One who can give you spiritual rest? Jesus said, "Come to Me." True physical rest comes only after one has experienced true spiritual rest in God through Jesus Christ. When you enjoy God's rest, you will have a firm foundation upon which to build for life as well as the reward of God's promised rest to look forward to when the road is hard or dark. When you answer Christ's call to come to Him, that's enough to interject peace and joy into your life.

✓ Have you evaluated your schedule lately? Are you so fixated on providing and making ends meet that perhaps you are not getting the proper rest? Or are you overdosing on social activities, late-night television, even church work?

Jesus' disciples overdid it in the area of ministry. And Jesus, knowing what was ahead and noticing His disciples' weariness, thought it important to take them away for a time of rest and recreation. And that time paid off! It was just what the doctor—correction: *the Savior!*—ordered. And God wants the same for you. Your life is not a sprint, but a marathon. Pace yourself! Remember, rest is important for a balanced life.

✓ How are you doing in the Vacation Department? No matter how comfortable you are with your work, you still need your rest and recreation. So be sure you take some time off. You will return to your daily routine with much more enthusiasm and, scientists say, with much more productivity.

✓ Have you cultivated any hobbies or interests that are totally unrelated to your job or your profession? These diversions provide a change of pace and engage your mind in new and different ways that help you to relax and be refreshed.

Elizabeth and I have learned to play chess and checkers together. We've also taken on some more physical hobbies such as walking, kayaking, and camping together. (And believe me, the more physical exertion your hobby requires, the better you rest at night!)

✓ Have you formed the habit of placing your daily burdens on the shoulders of your Savior? Worry, anxiety, and fear are burdens that Jesus will help you carry. Casting all your burdens and cares on Jesus will sweeten your life (1 Peter 5:7).

No horse gets anywhere
  until he is harnessed.
No steam or gas ever drives anything
  until it is confined.
No Niagara is ever turned into light and power
  until it is tunneled.
No life ever grows great
  until it is
        focused,
              dedicated,
                    disciplined.[28]

19

God's Powerful Promise of
Self-Discipline

I n order to manage our busy lives and accomplish any goals we have, we need one key trait: self-discipline. What's more, we need to work hard on developing self-discipline because God calls His people to cultivate this powerful trait. God expects His men and women to desire self-discipline, nurture it, and function by it.

There's no doubt about it—this is the character quality everyone loves to hate! But to do the work God calls us to do—whether at home, at work, at church, or on the mission field—we must incorporate self-discipline into our everyday life. In the words of the author of a book I try to read annually, we must "observe a soldierly discipline...so that [we] might wage a good warfare."[29] We as Christians have battles to fight...and win!

Now, let's dive in.

Meet Samson, one of the most promising men of his day. Samson's story is told in Judges 13–16. This man had everything going for him. An incredible destiny was waiting for him. What made Samson so special?

- Samson was selected by God, even while he was still in his mother's womb, to lead God's people during a time of great oppression (13:3-5).

- Samson was the "Mr. Universe" of his day. He had incredible strength. He once uprooted the city gates of a town and carried the gates and its posts more than 30 miles uphill (16:3). In addition, Samson could kill a lion with his bare hands (14:6)!

- Samson was the "poster boy" for the Special Forces of his day. He singlehandedly carried out numerous raids into enemy territory, inflicting heavy casualties (15:7-14).

- Samson was blessed with a godly heritage. Both of his parents witnessed a miraculous appearance of the angel of the Lord (13:20), and his mother carefully followed the instructions of the Lord during her pregnancy (13:4).

Yes, Samson possessed all the privileges that any person could ever want or need in order to be successful...except he lacked self-discipline! This character flaw caused him to become a tragic picture of runaway self-gratification, dissipation, and foolishness.

Discovering the Promise

It's been said, "Self-discipline does not make you great, but you cannot continue to be great without it." What is self-discipline? This term literally means "a calling to soundness of mind, or to self-control."[30] And friend, self-discipline—or the lack thereof!—is what separates a Samson from a Moses, or a man with mere potential from a man of power.

Samson knew he had everything, but he failed to use it for God's purposes. Later in the Bible we meet a man who was quite the opposite. His name is Timothy, and he thought he had nothing, yet he possessed everything.

Poor Timothy! His was a life filled with continual opposition. He was opposed because of his association with the apostle Paul. He was opposed because of the message of the gospel. Whatever the opposition, and to whatever the degree of that difficulty, Paul knew that this young minister- and man-in-the-making was struggling.

How was Timothy going to be able to handle all that was going on in his life? Would he timidly retreat from challenges, from ministry? Paul, the ever-present encourager, bolstered Timothy's confidence by reassuring him of God's powerful promise of self-discipline. "Father Paul" reminded young Timothy, his son in the faith, of God's power at work in his life. He passed on these words of promise and encouragement to "timid Timothy":

> *For God has not given us*
> *a spirit of timidity,*
> *but of power and love and discipline.*
> 2 TIMOTHY 1:7

Because of God's promise of discipline, Timothy could do the job he was called to do. God would empower him to control his thoughts and actions, and to discipline his attitudes, even under the most intense persecution and contention. What a promise! And friend, God is offering you this same promise.

Understanding the Promise

How can we acquire self-discipline? Understand that...

1. *Self-discipline involves your mind.*

Paul reminded Timothy that "God has not given us a spirit of timidity, but of power and love and discipline." God's promise of discipline included the idea of a secure and "sound mind" (NKJV):

- a mind that was disciplined,

- a mind that could understand the implications of proper and improper behavior, and

- a mind that had the ability to "think so as to have sound judgment" (Romans 12:3).

This is the kind of mental toughness that allows you to also experience success without becoming proud and to suffer failure without becoming defeated.

2. *Self-discipline involves your body.*

When you live a life of godly discipline, every area of your life is in its proper order—including your mind and body. As you well know, when you exercise self-discipline over your mind, it affects your body. You show restraint in what you eat and in how you act.

So that you can do your part in advancing the cause of Christ, both your mind and body need to be working in harmony. Just as you discipline your mind, you are to discipline your body. As Paul said, you are to "buffet" your body so that you don't become *its* slave, but rather, so your body becomes *your* slave (1 Corinthians 9:27).

3. Self-discipline has a "twin sister."

When God's Holy Spirit comes into your life at salvation, He brings a number of godly attitudes and traits with Him. (It's a good idea to read the entire list in Galatians 5:22-23—this will keep you on your toes!) One of these behaviors, or "fruit" as they are called, is self-control. As a believer, you have the Spirit's power within you to help you restrain your passions and appetites. You have the ability to say no to fleshly desires. The twin sister, self-control, will enable you to develop self-discipline.

4. Self-discipline is required in Scripture.

Like most godly attitudes that God requires of us, self-discipline does not come automatically. That's why you are required to "exercise...self-control in all things" (1 Corinthians 9:25). You are also required to "apply all diligence [and]...self-control" (2 Peter 1:5-6). How can you develop greater self-discipline?

— Walk by God's Spirit.

— Apply God's self-control in every situation.

— Do the work required of you to develop godly discipline.

Putting God's Power to Work

I am sure you want to live a life of productivity and accomplishment, right? So where can you begin? Start by identifying the areas of your life in which you need self-discipline. Here's a list...and feel free to add to it.

✓ *Spiritual life*—The starting point for living a life of self-control and self-discipline is evaluating your spiritual condition. Are you actively seeking to develop godly discipline? Are you successfully handling temptation? Are you dealing with sins such as anger, laziness... (only you know what to list)? Don't forget—unconfessed sin robs you of the spiritual power required to be self-disciplined.

✓ *Mental life*—Your mind is the control center for the rest of your body. Make sure you discipline your mind through the reading of God's Word. Memorize Scripture, especially verses dealing with the areas in which you need God's help to overcome weakness. And here's a big one! Discipline your mind away from stimuli that corrupt your thinking. Monitor what you see. Your eyes are the gateway to your mind. Like the computer slogan says so well, "G.I.G.O." When you put Garbage In, Garbage will come Out!

✓ *Physical life*—Just as your spiritual life requires your constant attention, so does your body. It is like a finely tuned car engine. Both the engine and your body need daily care to keep them working properly. So pay attention!

—Watch what, how often, and how much you eat.

—Get proper rest.

—Exercise on a regular basis.

—Say no to anything that impedes your desire for greater self-discipline.

✓   *Work life and home life*—Are you balancing these two areas of your life? Or are you spending an inordinate amount of time on your job? Are you neglecting your God-given priority to love your spouse and family? Both home and work are important. The wise Christian exercises discipline to keep these areas in balance.

✓   *Financial life*—One of the areas in which a lot of self-discipline and self-control is needed is in managing your money. Do you have a budget, and do you stick to it? Are you spending an excess on wants and not able to take care of needs? Are you guilty of buying on impulse? Are you giving God the "firstfruits" of your paycheck? Finances are a quick and sure way of determining your spiritual priorities...and the amount of self-discipline you have (or don't have!). What does your checkbook reveal?

The Nature of Discipline

— Discipline is a spiritual issue—*everything* done to the glory of God (1 Corinthians 10:31).

— Discipline has no shortcuts—no quick results.

— Discipline has no reserve—self-control must be reinstituted tomorrow.

— Discipline begins with the little things—like picking up your dirty clothes.

— Discipline tackles the difficult thing—easy requires little.

— Discipline starts with the mind—"I will."

— Discipline proceeds with a mandate—"I must."

— Discipline never gets distracted—"This one thing I do."

— Discipline never takes a vacation—it's for life.

— Discipline is ever-changing—growth requires new disciplines to meet life's next and latest challenges.[31]

He gives power to the tired and worn out,
and strength to the weak.
Even the youths shall be exhausted,
and the young men will all give up.
But they that wait upon the Lord
shall renew their strength.
They shall mount up with wings like eagles;
they shall run and not be weary;
they shall walk and not faint.
—Isaiah 40:29-31 TLB

God's Powerful Promise of
Strength

O ne evening I was flipping through the television chan-
nels looking for my favorite, The Weather Channel,
when I discovered the Power Team. I had heard about
these big guys before, but had never see them in action. So I
paused for a moment to get a better understanding of their out-
reach ministry.

In case you haven't heard of the Power Team, they are a
group of ex-jocks and body-builder types who tour the country
and share their testimonies about what it means to have faith
in Jesus Christ. These guys are incredible! They can break huge
blocks of concrete with their bare hands, just to name one of
their feats of strength. They are a team of Christian men who
use their physical strength to entertain and speak about their
love for Jesus.

Discovering the Promise

But these men are not the only ones who can be on a "power team." If you know and love Jesus, you, too, can be assured of God's promise of strength and power. Where can you get some of this strength, you ask? Here's the answer...and a promise of what God wants to do for you:

> *I can do all things*
> *through Christ who strengthens me.*
> PHILIPPIANS 4:13 NKJV

Now, let me quickly state that when you appropriate this promise of God's strength, you won't be able to break huge blocks of concrete! But God's kind of strength will allow you to be victorious in all areas of living the Christian life. That's better than breaking concrete blocks, don't you think?

Understanding the Promise

What a promise! "I can do all things through Christ who strengthens me." Now, what are some of the "all things"?

1. *Strength in every circumstance.*

The triumphant words of this promise come from the apostle Paul, and his confident reference to "all things" has to do with being in control in every circumstance. So whether Paul had a lot or a little, or whether he suffered a lot or a little, he was able to handle it, whatever "it" was. His attitude of "I can do all things" was the same in every circumstance (see Philippians 3:12).

Do you have any issues, any problems, any lacks, any "its" and "things" to deal with in your life? Then read on as Paul tells us how he made it through "all things."

The promise—The first half of this familiar verse declares a truth: "I can do all things," or "I can do everything" (NIV). This is the kind of message that you would expect to hear from a motivational speaker or a coach. It conveys the idea of self-reliance and self-assurance. It says, "*You* can do it! *You* can do anything you want to do if you put your mind to it."

Statements like these may be true in some areas of a person's life. Sure, given enough determination and willpower, you *can* accomplish a lot. But that's not what this verse is saying, when you consider the *source* of such power. So you must read on and finish Paul's message. He reveals that you "can do all things *through Christ,*" who strengthens you!

The source—Friend, *Christ* is the source of our strength. Don't miss it—it's *Christ! He* is the reason we can do the *all things* in the spiritual realm. How was Paul able to have this kind of optimistic perspective on the issues of life? It was because of Christ.

How often have you tried to live some aspect of your life in your own strength and ability? You had the skills. You had the know-how. Maybe you even had the money. But you tried to go it alone, without considering the Lord, to do it yourself. Well, how did you do?

I can make a pretty good guess, because I've been there and done that, too! I'm guessing you probably failed miserably. So the message is loud and clear—we must stop trusting in our own strength and abilities and instead rely on Christ and His strength.

2. *Strength for purity.*

There are many topics and issues both you and I could bring up that require Christ's strength for us to overcome. Right away we could list physical health, problems concerning jobs, the lack of together-time with family, a shortage of money. But sexual purity seems to be "The Big One"! Keeping our minds and bodies sexually pure is, as the titles of two popular books indicate, not only *Every Man's Battle* but also *Every Woman's Battle*.

Purity is a challenge, a daily struggle, a battle. But purity is God's will for you. His will is clearly stated: "This is the will of God, your sanctification; that is, that you abstain from sexual immorality; that *each of you* know how to possess his own vessel in sanctification and honor, not in lustful passion" (1 Thessalonians 4:3-5).

How then can we as men and women stay pure? The answer is simple yet powerful: *We can do all things through Christ who strengthens us.* If this area is a source of struggle for you (and remember, both of the book titles mentioned a moment ago included the word *every*), you must remember one thing: Draw on the source of *all* strength. Draw on the power of Jesus Christ, and fight your battle. You *can do all things*, even win the battle over sexual temptation, if—and only if—you allow Christ to give you His strength to overcome the temptation.

3. *Christian living.*

And so it goes! No matter what challenge you face or what circumstances—or temptations!—arise (and arise they will), God's powerful word of promise can be seized by every Christian. That's the truth of the Bible and God's promise to you. Christ's power is sufficient for any and all areas of our lives, period. What other areas are you struggling with in your Christian life? What about being a...

—☙— growing Christian

—◆— loving husband

—◆— supportive wife

—◆— caring parent or grandparent

—◆— faithful steward of God's resources

—◆— helpful friend

—◆— committed employee

—◆— humble servant

—◆— witness for Jesus

Do you think God wants any or all of these to be true about you? You know the answer, don't you? It's a resounding *yes!* God desires that you be doing all of the above—and more! Therefore, God has given you Jesus Christ. His strength will empower you to accomplish God's will.

Putting God's Power to Work

Do you desire God's strength at work in your life? If so (and I can't imagine why you wouldn't!), the following steps will get you started down the path of tapping into God's promised strength.

✓ *Abide in Christ*—Jesus put it this way: "I am the vine, you are the branches; He who abides in Me, and I in him, he bears much fruit; for apart from Me you can do nothing" (John 15:5). To receive power from Christ, you must stay closely connected to Him. If your union with Christ is strong, then the power of God will infuse and strengthen you to successfully face whatever challenges come your way. You can have strength for today's trials and tomorrow's challenges...as you abide in Christ.

Do whatever you must to stay close to the Power Source. Read your Bible daily and pray faithfully.

✓ *Be accountable to others*—The corollary of the principle of staying close to God is also true: If you allow your commitment to Jesus Christ, the Power Source, to wane, you will be powerless to handle the challenges and temptations that come your way. And come they will! Therefore, protect yourself from drifting by surrounding yourself with godly Christians. Find spiritual mentors who will check up on you in the areas in which you struggle.

✓ *Exercise your faith*—How do you grow in your physical strength? By exercising your body. And this principle is also true in the spiritual realm. You grow in spiritual strength by exercising your faith daily by...

—trusting God for the needs in your life

—praying and anticipating God's answers

—relying on God's strength in your weaknesses

—believing God's promises in your every trial

—being a consistent witness to your beliefs

—standing up for your faith

Friend, *you* can be on God's power team. You can tap into God's power through Jesus Christ. You already have God's promise of strength. Therefore, you "can do all things through Christ who strengthens" you! Now, act on this powerful truth from God. Exercise your faith in Christ, your Power Source!

The honor of this world doesn't last; it is transient; it is passing away, and I don't believe any man or woman is fit for God's service that is looking for worldly preferment, worldly honors, worldy fame. Let us get it under our feet, let us rise above it, and seek the honor that comes down from above.[32]

21

God's Powerful Promise of
Success

Imagine being successful in whatever you attempt. That would be great, wouldn't it? A successful business leader, creative artist, boss or employee, Bible teacher, husband, wife, or parent...the list could go on and on. Well, that seems to be the promise God made to one particular man many hundreds of years ago. And friend, that's the same promise God is offering to us today as well. Are you interested in being successful? Then read on.

Discovering the Promise

Joshua is the man I'm referring to. We've already looked at God's power in his life in our chapters on God's promise of courage and the promise of His presence. As you may remember, Joshua was the new leader of the nation of Israel. His former boss, Moses, had died. But before his death, Moses passed on the baton of leadership to Joshua. This had to be scary for Joshua! Moses was a great leader—no, Moses was one of *the greatest* leaders of all time! He had successfully guided the people of Israel—two million of them—out of Egypt, through the desert, to the border of a new land, the Promised Land.

It stands to reason that Joshua had every right to be a little nervous. How could he possibly fill Moses' sandals? It seemed like an impossible task! What advice could God give that would help encourage His new—and younger—leader? What was God's success-formula for Joshua some 3,000 years ago? (And let me add…God's success-formula for us today?)

> *This book of the law*
> *shall not depart from your mouth,*
> *but you shall meditate on it day and night,*
> *so that you may be careful to do*
> *according to all that is written in it;*
> *for then you will make your way prosperous,*
> *and then you will have success.*
> JOSHUA 1:8

Understanding the Promise

As you look at this promise that God wants to give, ask yourself, Does God's formula for success differ from mine? If you are like many people, you may measure success as achieving goals and prosperity, and gaining power and influence. But the strategy for gaining success that God gave to Joshua goes against everything the world would factor into a success-formula. Joshua followed God's strategy, and it sure worked for him!

- ‑∿‑ He was successful in the conquest of the land and its people. To this day, military strategists still study Joshua's approaches to battle.

- ‑∿‑ He was successful in the division of the land among the 12 tribes of Israel. This was no small task. Can you imagine trying to please two million new homeowners?

- ‑∿‑ He was successful and prosperous in his personal life. Joshua had been such a key person in the division of the land that the people rose up, as a group, and gave him a whole city as his allotment (Joshua 19:49).

As we noted at the beginning of this book, on many occasions God's promises come with conditions. And friend, this is one of those promises. Do you want to be successful in your everyday life by God's measurements? Then follow the conditions set forth in the success-formula as outlined for Joshua.

1. *Study God's Word constantly.*

Success in any area, whether it's corporate leadership or taking care of a home and tending a brood of kids, doesn't come easily. There is no such thing as instant success. Success for most people in any field of endeavor comes only after long hours and years of hard work. Charles M. Schwab, the great steel tycoon, is famous for his "Ten Commandments of Success." What was his Number-One commandment? Mr. Schwab put "hard work" at the top of the list. He explained, "Hard work is the best investment a man can make."

Here's another formula for success that points to the merits of hard work:

—∾— a 40-hour work week = survival

—∾— everything over 40 hours a week = success

When it comes to success in any and every undertaking, we would have to agree that there is no substitute for long days of hard work. And would you think it should be any different in the spiritual realm? It's the same process: To be successful in God's eyes, do as God told Joshua—"Study this book of the law continually" (NLT).

For Joshua, "this book of the law" was what had been handed down to him by Moses. These first five books of the Bible were all Joshua had to go by, but they were all that he would need. Today, besides the five books Joshua possessed, we also have 61 more books of the Bible to help us succeed in our Christian life and responsibilities. God promises us success, but here is one of the conditions: *You must study.* And herein lies the problem for many!

Please, don't "hate" to study. Don't think, *I gave up studying long ago—somewhere back in junior high or high school. I did only enough study to get by and get out of school…and now I'm done with that!* If you tend to cringe at the thought of studying, realize that a desire to *study* will help you succeed in your desire to *grow* spiritually. God's Word will strengthen you—as it did Joshua—as you face life's challenges. God values the study of His Word. He asks each believer to…

Be diligent [study, KJV]
to present yourself approved to God
as a workman who does not need to be ashamed,

handling accurately the word of truth.
2 TIMOTHY 2:15

Success at anything starts with
a desire for *knowledge*.

2. *Ponder God's Word continually.*

God asked Joshua to study His Word, and He also asked Joshua
to "meditate on it day and night." To *meditate* means "to read
with thoughtfulness, to linger over." This could also include
memorizing God's Word.

That was good advice to Joshua...and it's good advice to us.
Why? Because when we hear God's Word preached, we retain
about 10 percent of the message. When we read it, we retain
about 40 percent of what we read. But when we memorize
God's Word, we retain all—100 percent!—of its message to us.
As we mull over the Scriptures, we begin to better understand
what it is saying to us.

As a boy I was a member of a Bible club. I can still remember
the evening at church when I received an award for memorizing
600 verses from the Bible. But better than an award, I can still
recite many of the Bible passages I memorized as a child. They
are still mine...these many years later! No one—and nothing—
can take them away from me.

And here's another part of my story. Those verses were the
verses God used to turn my life around when I wasn't that interested in being successful in my Christianity. Those memorized
scriptures were so ingrained in my mind that I was constantly
confronted with their message to my wayward condition.

Do you want to be successful in your Christian life? In your
marriage? In your work? Do you want God's success-formula

close at hand, in your heart? Then do as Joshua did. Do as I did. And do as the psalmist who wrote these words did: "Your word I have hidden in my heart, that I might not sin against You" (Psalm 119:11 NKJV).

> Success at anything involves
> *understanding.*

3. *Apply God's Word completely.*

Application is the final ingredient in God's formula for success: "so that you may be *careful* to do everything written in it" (Joshua 1:8 NIV). This is no shallow reference to hit-or-miss application. These words describe accurate compliance and complete obedience—being "careful to do *every*thing written in it."

Successful people, male and female, will tell you that they became accomplished in their sport, business venture, role, fitness, hobby, profession, or whatever their areas of expertise by doing things correctly, and by not taking shortcuts. It doesn't matter how many times you swing a club or a racket, you are still going to send the ball in the wrong directions if you swing incorrectly. Mastery requires accuracy and follow-through.

And the same is true in the spiritual realm. We can do all sorts of religious activities—give money, pray, go to church, serve others, take Bible classes—but these won't make you successful unless you do them God's way. You must follow the rules! You must pay attention to what God's Word says... and apply it completely, accurately, diligently, and faithfully. Studying God's Word, memorizing it, and following it "to the letter" will help make your desires a reality.

Success at anything requires
precise *repetition*.

Putting God's Power to Work

Joshua's devotion to God is an inspiring example! He loved
God, and he loved God's Word. And he gives us a very straight-
forward lesson concerning God's desire for our success: If we
love God and follow Him and obey His Word, we will be successful—at least in the eyes of God—and that's all that matters!

How can you get this "success formula" going for you? Here
are a few steps for you to walk through:

✓ *Survey*...your heart and honestly assess those standards
   by which you may be judging success:

A good job?	A good marriage?
Your mate's job?	Lots of money?
Personal possessions?	A nice home?
A good education?	Social standing?
Lots of friendships?	Looks or fitness?
Your car?	

✓ *Surrender*...your understanding of how you have defined
   success, and then allow God to realign your values.

✓ *Search*...your heart and evaluate your level of obedience
   to God's Word. Have you been as careful as you should
   be in doing what the Bible says?

✓ *Surrender*...your ways, practices, and values that do
   not reflect the perspective and level of obedience God
   desires of you.

How can you enjoy the kind of success in your God-appointed assignments and battles that Joshua did in his? Or, put another way, where can you find the courage and hope of victory and the wisdom necessary for fulfilling your responsibilities? Joshua's faithfulness to God's careful instructions—to God's Word—shows us the way. Joshua was successful because he obeyed the rules. He did his part by carefully following God's formula as revealed in His Word. And God fulfilled His promise: "For then you will make your way prosperous, and then you will have success."

I am praying for you and your success as you follow the Lord!

From a life of sin and shame,
Into joy and peace I came,
Through the power of Jesus' name,
Into Victory!

From a path as dark as night,
Into glorious Gospel Light—
With a heart made pure and white,
Into Victory.[33]

22

God's Powerful Promise of
Victory

Recently a book about an undersized racehorse named Seabiscuit became a runaway bestseller. The book, written by Laura Hillenbrand, intertwines the lives of three men—the owner of the horse, the trainer, and the jockey—with the exploits of Seabiscuit, who beat all the odds time and time again, becoming a champion even after being sidelined with a crippling injury.

Seabiscuit became a symbol of triumph and victory over adversity and hopelessness to Depression-weary Americans during the 1930s and 1940s. Hillenbrand's book shows how the three men who guided Seabiscuit's destiny weathered hardships and endured the loss of loved ones and, in the end, were victorious in their personal lives.

Discovering the Promise

It's no wonder *Seabiscuit* is a best seller. It is a book with a message for every human heart and every need—a story of encouragement and hope! Packed with human drama and motivational content, *Seabiscuit* communicates to those who read it that, like the characters in the book, they, too, can be victorious over life's adversities.

But what if you and I could be part of another story, a story that shows how we can have victory in our personal life and then enjoy the *ultimate* victory—victory over death? Read on, because that's God's powerful promise to you!

> *Thanks be to God,*
> *who gives us the victory*
> *through our Lord Jesus Christ.*
> 1 Corinthians 15:57

Understanding the Promise

Victory is sometimes deceptive. Take the battles between General Ulysses Grant and Robert E. Lee as examples. Grant's forces suffered numerous defeats at the hands of Lee during the latter days of the Civil War. But ultimately, Grant was victorious.

Satan, our enemy, also seemed to be victorious in the Garden of Eden (Genesis 3), and even at the cross of Jesus. The Messiah was dead. It appeared as if all was lost, and Satan's control on humanity would remain firm. God seemed to be defeated.

But we all know that's not how the story ended, don't we? It didn't end with God's defeat. It never has...and it never will! No, it ended with Satan's defeat...and it always will! God was victorious. And "thanks be to God," you and I can now enter into God's "victory through our Lord Jesus Christ."

1. *Victory is certain.*

In this liberating promise, the apostle Paul is referring to the Christian's victory over death. He says, "Death is swallowed up into victory" (1 Corinthians 15:54). Physical death may present itself as final defeat, but it is only a slight "sting" (verse 55). That's all! Our victory over death is so certain that Paul gives thanks to God for having already accomplished that victory, for leading "us in His triumph in Christ" (2 Corinthians 2:14).

For several years I had the privilege of being the pastor to the seniors' class at my former church. During that period of time I witnessed and participated in numerous funerals. I spent a lot of time each week visiting hospitals and helping these dear folks deal with death and dying. Death was on the mind of every one of these older and still-aging senior citizens.

And I praise God that the vast majority of those senior saints were well assured of the fact that their deaths, even though they had not yet occurred, had already been "swallowed up in victory" through Jesus Christ. These brave, full-of-faith souls were ready for the future. Theirs was an attitude of "Go ahead, bring it on!" In fact, many yearned for heaven during the latter stages of their sufferings.

Now, let's get honest. Do you ever think about death? If you are like most people, regardless of your age, you think about death almost every day. Death is on your mind more than you would like to admit.

That's okay! Everyone needs to think about the future and about the reality of death and dying. But just as death is certain, so is Christ's victory over death...including *your* death! Yes, be concerned. And yes, be prepared and ready. But every day, even if you are fit as a fiddle and in the prime of life, be praising God for His "victory through our Lord Jesus Christ."

Friend, let's follow in Paul's pattern of praising God. Let's faithfully praise God for the certainty of His promise of victory. Praise lifts your eyes from the present battle to the future victory. "Thanks be to God," the power of death can no longer defeat!

2. *Victory is a gift.*

Have you ever repeatedly played against someone in a sport and never won a single game? Well, that was my experience during one of my two-week Army Reserve assignments. I was attached to an army hospital along with a doctor from my same army unit. Neither of us knew anyone else, so we spent most of our off-duty time together. Unfortunately for my doctor friend, he had no one else to play racquetball with, so he was forced to play with me. I had played racquetball only a few times in my life so, for two weeks, I was soundly defeated by a far superior player.

Well, that's a picture of our dilemma in the spiritual realm. You and all other Christians are incapable of defeating Satan, sin, and death on your own. But "thanks be to God" for the gift of victory! God has stepped in and conquered the enemy for us! God accomplished the victory, and now He "gives us the victory."

Do you realize what God's promise of victory over Satan, sin, and death means in your everyday life? It means that no matter how dark, difficult, discouraging, or frightening things may get or seem to be, you have hope! You have the assurance and hope that you are on the winning team...no matter what the present "score" is. Your side—God's side!—*will* win.

Friend, as life comes at you, you can have full peace of mind and heart. You can be like the person who reads the end of the book first. You already know how the story will end. You *know* that the victory is already yours. You have God's gift of hope, and His solid word of assurance of your victory. This should put a positive spin on everything you encounter or must endure. Such knowledge truly adds the silver lining to every cloud in life. Again, *thanks be to God* for the gift of His *victory!*

3. *Victory is because of Jesus.*

When Jesus rose from the dead, He conquered sin and death. Therefore, when we put our trust in Jesus, we experience victory "through our Lord Jesus Christ." His victory over death becomes our victory. God has given us eternal life through faith in His Son, the Lord Jesus. That's the ultimate victory! And as we've already seen in our chapter "God's Powerful Promise of...Life," that's something we can count on now. Knowing victory is certain removes a massive amount of fear and pressure from our lives.

> *If Christ is with us, who is against us?*
> *You can fight with confidence*
> *where you are sure of victory.*
> *With Christ and for Christ victory is certain.*[34]

I have a ritual I go through every time I travel. First, I leave behind a computer disk of my current writings, along with written instructions in the event of my death or a plane crash.

And then, periodically (and sometimes before each flight), I remind my wife of my love and remind her where everything is—wills, bank statements, life insurance policies—just in case.

Does this sound disturbing? Do you think this is morbid? Well, as I just said, we should all be prepared and ready for death...and I like to think that I am. But here's my reasoning: No one has foreknowledge of their exact time of death, but believers in Christ have assurance of eternal life—*thanks be to God!*—in the event of death.

That takes care of *death*. But what about victory over the struggles of *life?* We all face daily struggles with temptation all day every day of our lives. And that will be the case until we go to heaven. With Christ's victory and help, we can experience victory over the power of sin in daily life. All we need to do is put God's promise of victory to work.

We all worry and wonder about a long list of life-issues— losing our home, losing our children to the ways of the world, losing our job, income, and financial security, losing our health (and, as I said, you can add your worries to the list!). But the point is this: If Christ is Victor in your heart, then you can have His victory over *any* thing and *every* thing you will *ever* face in your *entire* life—period! That's what God wants to do for you!

Putting God's Power to Work

I have a saying that I try to remember when it comes to spiritual growth and change: "A problem defined is a problem half solved." It's a certainty you will always have "problem areas" in your life. Temptation is strong. And it's easy to develop bad habits. And habits are hard to conquer! Certainly these weaknesses give the enemy a strategic foothold in your life.

But again, *thanks be to God,* you no longer have to live in defeat in your pet problem area...or *any* area! God's powerful promise of victory extends to your life and your bad habits. Here's how you can begin to experience God's promised victory:

✓ *Acknowledge*...that your present spiritual setbacks are only skirmishes in your battle as you endeavor to walk with Christ. The enemy will have some victories in your life, but God has promised you ultimate victory because of your faith in Jesus Christ (1 John 5:4). It's a fact!

✓ *Affirm*...that your sin is an affront to the God who lives in you. And note—He is a "Holy, Holy, Holy" God (Isaiah 6:3)! Employ every necessary measure you can think of to deal with your sin.

✓ *Ask*...God for His forgiveness for each and every terrible affront to His holy character. And thank Him, at the same time, that He cleanses you of every unrighteousness in your life (1 John 1:9).

✓ *Acknowledge*...the strength and power of your enemy. Don't be ignorant. And don't be caught off guard! Satan is "the ruler of this world" (John 12:31). He is on the prowl "like a roaring lion," seeking someone to devour (1 Peter 5:8). Because Satan is such a powerful force, you must...

✓ *Allow*...God to empower you. He can enable you to do battle against temptation (2 Corinthians 12:9) and "against the rulers, against the powers, against the world forces of this darkness" (Ephesians 6:12).

✓   *Arm*...yourself with the Word of God. It must become your weapon of choice! It's "the sword of the Spirit" (Ephesians 6:17). With it firmly in hand, you can do ruthless battle against temptation, sin, and the enemy.

✓   *Avoid*...tempting situations. Don't even go to the scenes of temptation. And if and when temptation arises, run! Get out! Flee (2 Timothy 2:22)! Even a powerful force can be defeated if the battle is fought on the Bible's terms.

✓   *Account*...openly to others for your attitudes and actions. Be willing to allow others to hold you accountable and to pray for you (Proverbs 27:17).

With the help of God's Spirit, God's Word, and God's people, you can know victory in the war against the enemy. Regardless of the condition of the battle, you can give praise to the One who has made your ultimate victory possible.

*[Biblical] wisdom is always associated with
righteousness and humility
and is never found apart from
godliness and true holiness of life.*[35]
—A.W. TOZER

23

God's Powerful Promise of
Wisdom

On December 17, 1903, on a cold windy beach, five people and a dog watched history being made. The place was Kitty Hawk, North Carolina. The event was the first time that a heavier-than-air object had lifted off from the ground on its own power and made a sustained and controlled flight. This major event in history lasted just a few seconds, but the age of flight had begun! Orville Wright, age 32, piloted the *Flyer* as it was named, ten feet off the ground for 120 feet.

Later that same day, Wilbur, Orville's older brother, flew their plane a distance of 800 feet. The accomplishments of these two men represent a life of incurable optimism and dauntless labor and study. For years they had researched the efforts of others who had tried and failed. They had built and tested endless models before designing and building the *Flyer*.

Discovering the Promise

The wisdom that was needed to create this piece of history was the end result of long years of trial and error. But when it comes to your life, wouldn't it be faster and less painful to bypass the trials and errors and do things right the first time? To gain wisdom from the start?

Well friend, that's exactly what God wants to do in this next powerful promise. Do you want wisdom without the hit-and-miss efforts? God promises that if you ask for wisdom, you can have it. That's a powerful promise!

> *If any of you lacks wisdom,*
> *let him ask of God,*
> *who gives to all men generously*
> *and without reproach,*
> *and it will be given to him.*
> JAMES 1:5

Understanding the Promise

1. *Wisdom has its source in God.*

Everything has a source. It starts somewhere. Some years ago, our family was on vacation in Montana. While there, we drove over a short bridge with a sign that read, "Missouri River." We had been to St. Louis and seen the impressive width of the Missouri River just before it empties into the mighty Mississippi. This river in Montana, by contrast, was small. So we had to back up the car to make certain we hadn't misread the sign. Sure enough, it was the beginnings of the Missouri River. We weren't far from its source.

Now, everything has a source...except God. God *is* the

source of all things. You probably already know that the heavens and earth have their source in God (Genesis 1:1). But did you know that wisdom, too, has its source in God? God *is* wisdom (Ezra 7:25), and His wisdom and knowledge are derived from no one (Job 21:22). Therefore, all true wisdom has its source in God.

I admit I've been hammering away in every chapter about the need and the benefits of reading and studying your Bible. And now, you have another reason!

2. *Wisdom is more than knowledge.*

You've probably met some really smart people who impressed you at first but, as you got to know them a little better, you came to realize there wasn't much connection between their knowledge and their lives. Their lives were a mess! They lacked wisdom. On the other hand, there are many people who are "uneducated" by formal training standards, but they are wise in the decisions they make.

The *wisdom* that's written about in this promise requires no formal education. It is the proper application of knowledge. It is the ability to think clearly and make wise decisions, even in the midst of difficult situations and the emergencies of life. And friend, each of us *lacks wisdom!*

But good news! God is offering this kind of wisdom to us. He "gives [wisdom] to all men generously" to guide us in making right decisions through the tests and trials that come our way (James 1:2-4).

3. *Wisdom is available.*

Are you experiencing any problems or trials in your life? Are you at a crossroad in your career? Do you need direction in dealing with a family member or a friend? Are you struggling through some issues in your life? Or are you perhaps needing some help in the all-of-the-above category? Then you need wisdom—God's wisdom.

Well, what are you waiting for? God has promised you wisdom. He calls out, "If any of you lacks wisdom, let him ask of God."

Fellow Christian, you don't have to argue, debate, express your views and thoughts for days or weeks on end. And you don't have to grope around in the dark, hoping to stumble upon answers through trial and error. Whenever you need wisdom, you can pray to God, ask of God, and He will respond. It will be given to you!

4. *Wisdom is freely given.*

Have you ever had to ask for a loan? The loan officer probably took a lot of time with your application. He may have exercised such great caution you began to think it was his own money he was lending you! Having to make such a request can be agony. If you are like me, you probably walked out of that bank hoping you would never have to go through that experience again.

God's response to your request for wisdom is just the opposite. He "gives to all men generously." God doesn't dole out wisdom a little here and a little there. And He doesn't give it grudgingly. He *gives* "to all" who ask. And He gives His wisdom freely, liberally, generously.

God also doesn't give a lecture every time you come to Him asking, "More wisdom, please." No, each time you ask, wisdom is given "without reproach." With this kind of promise, and with this kind of freedom, why, oh why, aren't we all beating a path to God on a more regular basis?

5. *Wisdom comes in a variety of ways.*

As I said earlier, God is the source of wisdom. Now, while the Missouri River has one source, it has many tributaries that add to its size and power as it flows toward its destiny, the mighty Mississippi. What "wisdom tributaries" does God feed into your life to strengthen and mature you to make you wise?

— A worshipful attitude—Wisdom comes as you develop a worshipful attitude toward God. The foundation of wisdom is to "fear the Lord" (Proverbs 1:7). As you honor and esteem God, live in awe of His power, and obey His Word, His wisdom becomes your wisdom. It's yours as you allow Him to become the controlling influence in your life.

  Here's wisdom for you: Attending church regularly helps you to nurture such an attitude. Why do you go to church? To worship.

— The Word of truth—God's Word can make you wise—wiser than your enemies, your teachers, even those older and more experienced than you. How can you get this wisdom? All you have to do is love God's Word, hold it first in your heart and mind, and obey it (Psalm 119:98-100).

  Here's wisdom for you: Going through a devotional will help you get into the Bible. As you look to God's Word daily, it will make a difference in your life.

— The wisdom of others—You can gain wisdom through seeking the advice of those who possess wisdom. Watch their lives. Ask them questions. You can also read the wise and godly advice of others through Christian books.

In either case, you are learning and growing as you seek the wisdom of others.

Here's wisdom for you: Pray for mentors. Ask God who might be available to help you. Ask if you can get together to talk. And pay a visit to your Christian bookstore. See what books are available that can help you grow in wisdom.

Putting God's Power to Work

What should we as Christians want to be? Answer: A man or a woman of wisdom! And what steps must we take to become a wise man or woman?

✓ *You must desire wisdom*—And you must want it above all else. Solomon shows us this heart-attitude. He was given a choice to have anything he wanted. God said, "Ask what you wish Me to give you." What was Solomon's reply? He asked for wisdom—for "an understanding heart" (1 Kings 3:5,9).

Wisdom is the best trait to desire. As Solomon teaches, "How blessed is the man who finds wisdom, and the man who gains understanding. For its profit is better than the profit of silver, and its gain than fine gold" (Proverbs 3:13-14).

A few questions for you: How do the desires of your heart measure up? Do you wish for riches and a long life? Or do you wish for wisdom? Do some soul-searching right now. Are you seeking the world's answers to true happiness?

✓ *You must pray for wisdom*—Our promise in this chapter says that you are to *ask*. How do you "ask of God"?

Through prayer. Prayer acknowledges your dependence on God. And since your wisdom is short-term and in short supply, you need to be constantly asking God for His wisdom for your life.

A few questions for you: How's your prayer life? Most men have plenty of time to read the sports section of the newspaper, while many women soak up information in magazines. But somehow prayer isn't worked into their busy schedules. Is prayer slotted into your appointment book? And remember, you don't have to break any records for the longest prayer session! Just humbly bow your head...and ask for wisdom.

✓ *You must seek wisdom*—Wisdom is promised, but wisdom must also be sought after. Wisdom calls, but you must answer the call. To discover the treasure of wisdom, you must follow God's treasure map: "For *the Lord* gives wisdom. From *His mouth* come knowledge and understanding" (Proverbs 2:6).

A few questions for you: Once again, how is your Bible-reading time? Nonexistent? Doing better? Needing improvement? God's wisdom is in His Word. And God says you are to "seek [wisdom] as silver, and search for her as for hidden treasure" (Proverbs 2:4).

✓ *You must continue to nurture wisdom*—Wisdom is not permanent. And wisdom does not perpetuate itself. Wisdom must be sought day after day. Your gift of God's wisdom is for today. Use it with God's blessings, but don't count on today's wisdom for tomorrow's needs. Tomorrow you must get up and seek it again. Seek it by all the same means (prayer, Bible study, and wise counsel) that you used to acquire it today. Your life is constantly changing, and today's wisdom will not be adequate for the issues that you will face tomorrow. To continue to be a wise person, you must nurture wisdom continually.

A few questions for you: Earlier in this book I mentioned Aquila and Priscilla, the couple who assisted the apostle Paul and the church in numerous ways. And noted this about them: When they heard the mighty Apollos teach, "they took him aside and explained to him the way of God more accurately" (Acts 18:26). How do you think Aquila and Priscilla grew spiritually to the point of knowing and discerning God's truth? And how do you think you can do this as well? Are you committed to praying for, seeking, and nurturing God's wisdom? If you are, you will possess the world's greatest treasure!

For You formed my inward parts;
You covered me in my mother's womb.
I will praise You,
for I am fearfully and wonderfully made;
marvelous are Your works,
and that my soul knows very well.
—Psalm 139:13-14 NKJV

24

God's Powerful Promise of
Worth

There's no doubt Leo Tolstoy is one of the world's most renowned authors. Almost everyone has heard of his novel *War and Peace*, which was published in 1886. Tolstoy was born into a privileged aristocratic family, so he didn't have to worry about survival like most of the other children his age did while growing up in Russia during the early nineteenth century.

But Tolstoy did have his personal struggles as a child and an adolescent. He wrestled with what most young boys and girls and many adults struggle with in our day and age—a sense of worth. Because of his low personal estimation of his physical appearance, Tolstoy at one point in his life begged God to work a miracle and transform him into a handsome man. (Sounds a lot like the kind of request many people would make today, doesn't it?)

Not until years later, as an adult, did Tolstoy realize that external looks are not what gives a person worth. In some of his writings, Tolstoy revealed his discovery that inner beauty and a strong character are what pleases God the most, and therefore are what is most important. It appears that with this shift of focus in Tolstoy's thinking came something of a rebirth in his life.

Once Tolstoy's mind and heart came to recognize what is truly important in life, his writings evidenced a new sense of passion and purpose. His characters took on a more courageous and confident nature, a reflection of Tolstoy's new personal confidence.

Discovering the Promise

Like Tolstoy, many men and women today suffer from what has been labeled by some as low self-esteem or low self-image. In their minds, there is something wrong with them. They are too tall...too short...too large...too whatever. Some who fail to understand their worth handle it by withdrawing into a shell of sadness and loneliness. Others try to compensate in some other way, such as putting on a mask of self-assurance—a boisterous, loud, life-of-the-party facade. It is no wonder that so many folks have problems with self-respect when they place their entire focus on "self"!

But what if you and I take a different perspective and talk about our worth in God's eyes? Or our worth in Jesus Christ? Here's God's answer to the self-esteem problem as given in this powerful promise from Jesus:

> *Are not two sparrows sold for a cent?*
> *And yet not one of them will fall to the ground*
> *apart from your Father.*
> *But the very hairs of your head are all numbered.*
> *Therefore do not fear;*
> *you are of more value than many sparrows.*
> MATTHEW 10:29-31

Understanding the Promise

When Jesus declared this comforting statement, He was in the midst of assuring His disciples that no matter what happened in the future as they preached the gospel, they could be courageous and confident. Why? Because of their connection to God and their worth to the Father and His concern for them.

1. *Your worth is measured by God's sovereign care.*

Jesus masterfully drove His point home: Even when a single, seemingly insignificant sparrow falls to the ground, it does not happen "apart from your Father," or apart from the Father's knowledge. Jesus reasoned that if God is this concerned about *one* sparrow, how much more do you think He is concerned about you? And the answer? More! Much more! Jesus said "you are of more value than many sparrows."

And Jesus didn't stop there! You are so important to your Father that He has numbered "the very hairs of your head." Medical experts estimate there are more than 100,000 hair follicles on the human scalp, and that the average man loses—and sprouts—about 100 hairs a day. (Unfortunately, the experts "forgot" to mention the number of women's hair follicles, but it is probably similar! Nevertheless...) It's truly amazing. God has your every hair numbered. That's how important you are to Him! Why would you ever doubt your God-given worth and your significance to Him?

2. *Your worth is determined by your closeness to Jesus.*

Some people suffer from a low self-image because they erroneously think they aren't worth anything. Others have just the opposite problem. They have a huge ego. They think there is nothing they can't do. They think they are worth everything! Notice that both those with low self-esteem and those with big egos have their focus on *themselves* and their own abilities or lack of abilities.

But as a Christian, you must know that your worth comes from Jesus Christ. He said, "I am the vine, you are the branches; he who abides in Me, and I in him, he bears much fruit; for apart from Me you can do nothing" (John 15:5). Friend, the basis of your worth is your identity in and with Christ! It's that simple. Apart from Him, you are incapable, by eternal standards, of accomplishing very much. Oh, many men and women think they are successful. That's because they have measured their success with human eyes and by human standards (annual salary, square footage of their home, education, job, talent, professional standing). But true worth comes only when you abide in Christ and stay closely connected with Him. Jesus alone is truly worthy, and it is in Him, in Christ, that you possess your worth.

3. *Your worth is grounded in creation.*

Early in our marriage, Elizabeth and I created a pine bookcase. Elizabeth drew up the design, and I built it, cutting the pieces of wood and fitting them together. Then we stained our "work of art." For the next 30 years, that bookcase was the focal point in our family room. It was practically worthless, costing only about $30 in materials...except that *we* had made it. That made it priceless to us.

The human body is made up of materials worth only a few cents. But to God, you are priceless. Why? Because He created you. "God created man in His own image...male and female He created them" (Genesis 1:27). Just as our pine bookcase is special to us, so God has declared that you are special to Him. Doesn't it follow that if you are priceless to the God of the universe, you should not have any feelings of worthlessness? You should never think yourself worthless or useless if you claim a relationship to the great God who made you.

Putting God's Power to Work

God has promised that you are valuable to Him. He created you. He sovereignly cares for you. And He reinforces your worth as you stay close to His Son and your Savior. So what can you do to help remember your worth in Christ?

✓   *Thank God*...that He created you exactly the way you are (regardless of the number of hairs that are or aren't on your head!). It's a fact: You are "fearfully and wonderfully made" (Psalm 139:14)...and God never makes a mistake! You will be strengthened when you believe this truth.

✓   *List*...whatever limitations you think you have. Then thank God for each one. Your limitations force you to trust God. You must depend on Him and His strength in the areas of your weaknesses. If God chooses not to remove your limitations, He promises to increase your strength to bear them: "My grace is sufficient for you, for

My strength is made perfect in weakness" (2 Corinthians 12:9 NKJV).

✓ *Determine*...if there are steps you can take to minimize, improve, or eliminate your limitations. Do you need more schooling? Do you need to shed a few pounds? Do you need to learn better communication skills? Better organizational skills?

✓ *Realize*...that any and all limitations are for your good (Romans 8:28) and God's glory. Accept them and glory in them. You must learn that...

> the Lord has more need of our weakness than of our strength: our strength is often His rival; our weakness, His servant, drawing on His resources, and showing forth His glory.[36]

God's Promises
and Your Character

Wouldn't it be nice if you could count on people to come through on their promises? Most likely, you've been burned and disappointed by people who failed to keep their word.

A Personal Story

Have you had an experience similar to what happened to Elizabeth and me this past week? A salesperson was trying to persuade us to buy a particular writing desk. It was a beautiful desk that we just knew would inspire us to write a best seller or two. But there was only one problem—the desk was a *writing* desk and didn't have a place for a computer keyboard.

"No problem!" said the salesperson. "I know a cabinetmaker

who can convert the middle drawer into a tray for your keyboard. I'll call him up, and while you are away on your speaking tour, I'll have him make the drawer work."

Sounded good to us! So, with this person's promise ringing in our ears, we purchased the desk and arranged to have it delivered.

Well, you can probably guess the rest of our story. We arrived back home from a trip...to find that nothing had been done about the desk drawer. Now, you may be thinking that this is "small potatoes" compared to a particular promise that was broken to you. And you know, you're probably right. But our insignificant plight illustrates the importance of kept promises, whether big or small.

A Word of Encouragement

Dear friend, as we prepare to part our ways, and to go on to experience more of what God wants to do in our lives, let me leave you with this truth—

The power of a promise
depends on
the one making the promise.

Now, contrast our disappointing experience with a salesperson's word with the trustworthiness of God's Word and His promises to us. Remember what I have repeated throughout this book: God always keeps His promises to us, and God cannot lie or be unfaithful. Therefore...

✓   You can always count on God.

✓   You can always believe in God's Word.

✓   You can always depend on God's nature.

✓   You can always rely on God's power.

✓   You can always trust in God's promises.

A Word of Challenge

Now about that desk…. The promise made to us had no power. Why? Because of a flaw in the character, or the ability, of the person making the promise. Surely the salesperson sincerely meant to follow through. And surely, something critical must have occurred to distract her, or to limit her, from fulfilling her promise to us.

But, whether she meant to follow through or not, because of the broken promise, her character, unfortunately, is in question. The salesperson may have had good intentions…but we now have a beautiful desk that is less than satisfactory because of an unfulfilled promise.

Here's the challenge: You (and I) mirror God's nature or character when you keep your word and your promises to others. If you are going to make a promise, whether that promise is made to your marriage partner, your children, a fellow church member, your boss or a workmate, or anyone else, be sure you keep it. Your character is at stake!

Study Guide

God's Powerful Promises to You

As you read in the prologue, what meant the most to you or encouraged your faith in God?

What truths or insights deepened your understanding of the character of God?

What presented the greatest challenge in your daily life?

The chapter sections that are listed below deal with the
nature of God's powerful promises. As you reflect on
their content, write down what impressed you the most from
each section. Begin by reading 1 Kings 8:56 in your Bible and
copying it here.

The Nature of a Promise—

The Nature of God—

The Nature of Promises in the Bible—

The Nature of God's Promises to You—

Which suggestions, activities, or questions regarding God's powerful promises do you think would make the greatest difference in your life, and why?

What can you do to make your answer(s) a reality?

LESSON 1

As you read in the preceding chapter, what meant the most to you or encouraged your faith in God?

What truths or insights deepened your understanding of the character of God?

What presented the greatest challenge in your daily life?

Discovering the Promise

Read Matthew 7:7-8 in your Bible. Copy it here.

What is your role?

What is God's promise?

How does this encourage you to pray?

Understanding the Promise

Look again at the nine reasons we don't pray more often. Also read each Scripture reference in your Bible. What is your Number One reason for not praying? Please explain.

Applying the Promise

Which suggestions, activities, or questions regarding answered prayer do you think would make the greatest difference in your life, and why?

What can you do to make your answer(s) a reality?

LESSON 2

As you read in the preceding chapter, what meant the most to you or encouraged your faith in God?

What truths or insights deepened your understanding of the character of God?

What presented the greatest challenge in your daily life?

Discovering the Promise

Read 2 Corinthians 5:17 in your Bible. Copy it here.

What is the promise?

What is the condition of this promise?

What is the result of being in Christ?

Understanding the Promise

Read the verses below and briefly note what they teach about the process of spiritual growth and change.

Ephesians 4:14-15—

Philippians 3:12-14—

1 Peter 2:2—

2 Peter 3:18—

Consider the four facts about the process of change. Which one do you need to remember as you grow spiritually, and why?

Applying the Promise

Which suggestions, activities, or questions regarding change do you think would make the greatest difference in your life, and why?

What can you do to make your answer(s) a reality?

LESSON 3

As you read in the preceding chapter, what meant the most to you or encouraged your faith in God?

What truths or insights deepened your understanding of the character of God?

What presented the greatest challenge in your daily life?

Discovering the Promise

Read 2 Corinthians 1:3-4 in your Bible. Copy it here.

How is God described in this promise?

What does God do for His people?

How does your experience and God's comfort help you help others?

Understanding the Promise

Read the verses below and note what they teach about God and His comfort.

Psalm 23:4—

Psalm 147:3—

Matthew 5:4—

2 Corinthians 1:5—

How does the promise of God's comfort help you in any current afflictions?

Applying the Promise

Which suggestions, activities, and questions regarding comfort do you think would make the greatest difference in your life, and why?

What can you do to make your answer(s) a reality?

LESSON 4

As you read in the preceding chapter, what meant the most to you or encouraged your faith in God?

What truths or insights deepened your understanding of the character of God?

What presented the greatest challenge in your daily life?

Discovering the Promise

Read Philippians 1:6 in your Bible. Copy it here.

What has God done in your life?

What does God promise to do in your life?

How long will His promise be in effect?

Understanding the Promise

Review the three truths presented in the chapter and the scriptures below. Note what is involved in God's work of completion in you.

1. God's work in your salvation—John 1:12

2. God's work in us—1 Corinthians 1:2

3. God's work for us—Romans 8:28-29

Applying the Promise

Which suggestions, activities, or questions regarding completion do you think would make the greatest difference in your life, and why?

What can you do to make your answer(s) a reality?

LESSON 5

As you read in the preceding chapter, what meant the most to you or encouraged your faith in God?

What truths or insights deepened your understanding of the character of God?

What presented the greatest challenge in your daily life?

Discovering the Promise

Read Joshua 1:9 in your Bible. Copy it here.

What was God's exhortation to Joshua?

What was God's caution to Joshua?

What was God's promise to Joshua?

Understanding the Promise

Read Joshua 1:1-9.

Why should the knowledge of God's presence give Joshua courage?

Why do you think this promise was important to Joshua?

Why is it important to you?

How does Psalm 23:4 give you courage?

Applying the Promise

Which suggestions, activities, or questions regarding courage do you think would make the greatest difference in your life, and why?

What can you do to make your answer(s) a reality?

LESSON 6

As you read in the preceding chapter, what meant the most to you or encouraged your faith in God?

What truths or insights deepened your understanding of the character of God?

What presented the greatest challenge in your daily life?

Discovering the Promise

Read 1 Corinthians 10:13 in your Bible. Copy it here.

List at least four truths presented in this powerful promise.

What promise(s) do you see in this verse?

Understanding the Promise

What do you learn about God from 1 Corinthians 10:13?

What do you learn about temptation?

What do you learn about deliverance...

...from David's life in 2 Samuel 11:1-4?

...from Joseph's life in Genesis 39:1-12?

Applying the Promise

Which suggestions, activities, or questions regarding deliverance do you think would make the greatest difference in your life, and why?

What can you do to make your answer(s) a reality?

LESSON 7

As you read in the preceding chapter, what meant the most to you or encouraged your faith in God?

What truths or insights deepened your understanding of the character of God?

What presented the greatest challenge in your daily life?

Discovering the Promise

Read Psalm 103:12 in your Bible. Copy it here.

What is God's promise?

How extensive is His promise?

Understanding the Promise

Write out the five descriptions of God's forgiveness.

—

—

—

—

—

Which of these descriptions gave you the greatest encouragement? Check it, and share why.

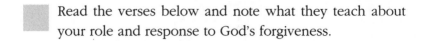 Read the verses below and note what they teach about your role and response to God's forgiveness.

Ephesians 4:32—

1 John 1:9—

Applying the Promise

Which suggestions, activities, or questions regarding forgiveness do you think would make the greatest difference in your life, and why?

What can you do to make your answer(s) a reality?

Lesson 8

As you read in the preceding chapter, what meant the most to you or encouraged your faith in God?

What truths or insights deepened your understanding of the character of God?

What presented the greatest challenge in your daily life?

Discovering the Promise

Read 2 Corinthians 12:9 in your Bible. Copy it here.

Read 2 Corinthians 12:8. Who is stating this promise?

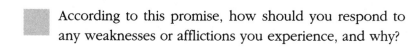 According to this promise, how should you respond to any weaknesses or afflictions you experience, and why?

Understanding the Promise

Write out three truths about God's grace.

1.

2.

3.

Read the verses below and note what they teach about God's grace.

2 Corinthians 9:8—

Ephesians 2:8—

2 Peter 3:18—

How has your understanding of God's grace been
enriched?

Applying the Promise

Which suggestions, activities, or questions regarding God's
grace do you think would make the greatest difference in
your life, and why?

What can you do to make your answer(s) a reality?

LESSON 9

As you read in the preceding chapter, what meant the most to you or encouraged your faith in God?

What truths or insights deepened your understanding of the character of God?

What presented the greatest challenge in your daily life?

Discovering the Promise

Read Proverbs 3:5-6 in your Bible. Copy it here.

What is your "triple" role?

What is God's promise?

Understanding the Promise

Think about how you normally make decisions. Then review the three instructions in the chapter. Which is the most difficult for you, and why?

Read the following verses and note what they teach about God's guidance.

Psalm 37:4-5—

Proverbs 3:7—

Matthew 6:33—

Acts 9:6—

Applying the Promise

Which suggestions, activities, or questions regarding guidance do you think would make the greatest difference in your life, and why?

What can you do to make your answer(s) a reality?

LESSON 10

As you read in the preceding chapter, what meant the most to you or encouraged your faith in God?

What truths or insights deepened your understanding of the character of God?

What presented the greatest challenge in your daily life?

Discovering the Promise

Read Jeremiah 29:11 in your Bible. Copy it here.

What do you learn about God?

What do you learn about His plans for you?

Understanding the Promise

Look at this section again. Write out the three anchors of your hope. Note the one you need to hold on to now, and why.

1.

2.

3.

Read the verses below and note how they encourage you and give you hope for the future.

Psalm 23:6—

Romans 8:28—

Titus 3:7—

Applying the Promise

Which suggestions, activities, or questions regarding hope do you think would make the greatest difference in your life, and why?

What can you do to make your answer(s) a reality?

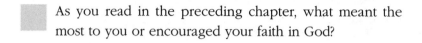

LESSON 11

As you read in the preceding chapter, what meant the most to you or encouraged your faith in God?

What truths or insights deepened your understanding of the character of God?

What presented the greatest challenge in your daily life?

Discovering the Promise

Read John 10:10 in your Bible. Copy it here.

Contrast Jesus' promise with the actions of a thief.

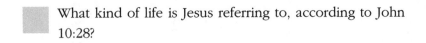 What kind of life is Jesus referring to, according to John 10:28?

Understanding the Promise

Write out the three truths about life in Christ.

1.

2.

3.

Read the verses below and note what they teach about "life."

John 3:15-16—

John 6:40—

John 11:25-26—

John 14:6—

John 20:31—

Are you presently reveling in the abundance of the eternal life Jesus secured for you? In what ways?

Applying the Promise

Which suggestions, activities, or questions regarding life do you think would make the greatest difference in your life, and why?

What can you do to make your answer(s) a reality?

Lesson 12

As you read in the preceding chapter, what meant the most to you or encouraged your faith in God?

What truths or insights deepened your understanding of the character of God?

What presented the greatest challenge in your daily life?

Discovering the Promise

Read 2 Timothy 1:7 in your Bible. Copy it here.

What response to life's problems does not come from God? (See also 1 John 4:18.)

What has God promised and provided instead? (See also 1 John 4:8.)

Understanding the Promise

Read Romans 8:39. How should this truth further strengthen your confidence in God's promise of love?

Review the four truths in the chapter. Then read the verses that follow and note what they teach you about God's love.

Romans 5:5—

Galatians 5:22—

1 John 4:19—

Read 1 Corinthians 13:4-8. How are you demonstrating—
or not demonstrating—love to others?

Applying the Promise

Which suggestions, activities, or questions regarding love
do you think would make the greatest difference in your
life, and why?

What can you do to make your answer(s) a reality?

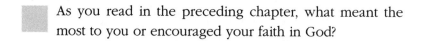

LESSON 13

As you read in the preceding chapter, what meant the most to you or encouraged your faith in God?

What truths or insights deepened your understanding of the character of God?

What presented the greatest challenge in your daily life?

Discovering the Promise

Read John 14:27 in your Bible. Copy it here.

Read John 14:23. Who is offering this peace?

How is this peace described by Jesus?

What admonishment was given with the promise?

Understanding the Promise

Read Luke 8:22-25. How would you rate the anxiety level of the disciples on a scale of 1 to 5 (1 being completely at peace, and 5 being a panic attack)?

1   2   3   4   5

What trial are you presently experiencing? How would you rate your anxiety level on a scale of 1 to 5?

1   2   3   4   5

Read Psalm 56:3-4. What was David's secret to handling stressful situations?

Applying the Promise

Which suggestions, activities, or questions regarding peace do you think would make the greatest difference in your life, and why?

What can you do to make your answer(s) a reality?

Lesson 14

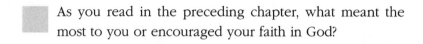

As you read in the preceding chapter, what meant the most to you or encouraged your faith in God?

What truths or insights deepened your understanding of the character of God?

What presented the greatest challenge in your daily life?

Discovering the Promise

Read Acts 1:8 in your Bible. Copy it here.

Read Acts 1:9-10. Who made this promise?

What was the source of the promised power?

What would result from this power?

Understanding the Promise

Read the following verses and note what they teach about power and the Holy Spirit.

Acts 1:8—

Ephesians 1:13—

2 Corinthians 12:9—

1 Corinthians 12:7—

Applying the Promise

Which suggestions, activities, or questions regarding power do you think would make the greatest difference in your life, and why?

What can you do to make your answer(s) a reality?

LESSON 15

As you read in the preceding chapter, what meant the most to you or encouraged your faith in God?

What truths or insights deepened your understanding of the character of God?

What presented the greatest challenge in your daily life?

Discovering the Promise

Read Joshua 1:9 in your Bible. Copy it here.

Read Joshua 1:1-9.

—Who is making this promise (verse 1), and what did He "command" Joshua to do (verse 2)?

—What else was promised to Joshua (verses 3-4)?

—What was Joshua to do (verses 6-9), and what would God do (verses 5 and 9)?

Understanding the Promise

Read the following verses and note what they teach about God's presence.

Matthew 28:20—

Hebrews 13:5-6—

Psalm 139:7-10—

How does the promise of God's presence encourage you?

Applying the Promise

Which suggestions, activities, or questions regarding presence do you think would make the greatest difference in your life, and why?

What can you do to make your answer(s) a reality?

LESSON 16

As you read in the preceding chapter, what meant the most to you or encouraged your faith in God?

What truths or insights deepened your understanding of the character of God?

What presented the greatest challenge in your daily life?

Discovering the Promise

Read Philippians 4:19 in your Bible. Copy it here.

What is the promise?

Who is the source of the promised provision?

What was the source of the promised provision?

Understanding the Promise

Read the following verses and note what they teach about God's provision.

Psalm 23:1—

Psalm 37:25—

Matthew 6:31-33—

2 Corinthians 9:8—

Read Hebrews 4:16 and record its instruction regarding your needs.

Applying the Promise

Which suggestions, activities, or questions regarding provision do you think would make the greatest difference in your life, and why?

What can you do to make your answer(s) a reality?

LESSON 17

As you read in the preceding chapter, what meant the most to you or encouraged your faith in God?

What truths or insights deepened your understanding of the character of God?

What presented the greatest challenge in your daily life?

Discovering the Promise

Read Jeremiah 1:5 in your Bible. Copy it here.

—How far back in time did God's knowledge of Jeremiah's purpose extend? At what point in time did God "consecrate" or "set apart" Jeremiah for his purpose of prophetic ministry?

—Who took full credit and responsibility for Jeremiah's purpose and calling?

Understanding the Promise

Read the following verses, and note what they teach about God's purposes and your life.

Ephesians 2:10—

2 Timothy 1:9—

1 Corinthians 12:4-7 and 11—

God is your rightful owner and has the right to employ you and make use of you as He pleases. How does this impact your life?

Applying the Promise

Which suggestions, activities, or questions regarding purpose do you think would make the greatest difference in your life, and why?

What can you do to make your answer(s) a reality?

Lesson 18

As you read in the preceding chapter, what meant the most to you or encouraged your faith in God?

What truths or insights deepened your understanding of the character of God?

What presented the greatest challenge in your daily life?

Discovering the Promise

Read Matthew 11:28 in your Bible. Copy it here.

Read Matthew 11:25-29.

Who is issuing this invitation and promise (verse 25), and how does He describe Himself (verse 29)?

To whom was the call and the promise extended?

What is the promise?

Read Matthew 11:29-30 and note the additional information and requirements regarding the promise.

Understanding the Promise

Review this section again. What did you learn about rest as...

...a part of God's plan?

...a gift of God?

...a part of a balanced life?

Applying the Promise

Which suggestions, activities, or questions regarding rest do you think would make the greatest difference in your life, and why?

What can you do to make your answer(s) a reality?

LESSON 19

As you read in the preceding chapter, what meant the most to you or encouraged your faith in God?

What truths or insights deepened your understanding of the character of God?

What presented the greatest challenge in your daily life?

Discovering the Promise

Read 2 Timothy 1:7 in your Bible. Copy it here.

What emotion or character flaw was apparently causing problems in Timothy's life and ministry?

List the three spiritual resources God promises and provides.

—

—

—

Read the following verses and note how the Holy Spirit
helps us to manifest the same qualities listed in this
promise.

Acts 1:8—

Romans 5:5—

Galatians 5:22-23—

Understanding the Promise

Read the following verses and note how self-discipline and self-restraint apply to daily life.

1 Timothy 2:9—

1 Timothy 2:15—

1 Timothy 3:2—

Titus 2:2—

Titus 2:3—

Titus 2:4-5—

Titus 2:6—

Titus 2:12—

What impacts you when you realize the importance of self-discipline in every area of your life and ministry?

Applying the Promise

Which suggestions, activities, or questions regarding self-discipline do you think would make the greatest difference in your life, and why?

What can you do to make your answer(s) a reality?

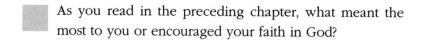

LESSON 20

As you read in the preceding chapter, what meant the most to you or encouraged your faith in God?

What truths or insights deepened your understanding of the character of God?

What presented the greatest challenge in your daily life?

Discovering the Promise

Read Philippians 4:13 in your Bible. Copy it here.

What is the truth declared in this verse?

What is the power source behind the statement?

Read Philippians 4:11-12. What are some of the "things" the apostle Paul discovered he could "do" because of this powerful promise?

Understanding the Promise

What is your greatest challenge today? How does God's promise of strength encourage you in this difficulty?

Read the following verses and note in a few words what they add to your understanding of God's strength in your life.

2 Corinthians 12:9—

Ephesians 3:16—

Colossians 1:11—

Applying the Promise

Which suggestions, activities, or questions regarding strength do you think would make the greatest difference in your life, and why?

What can you do to make your answer(s) a reality?

LESSON 21

As you read in the preceding chapter, what meant the most to you or encouraged your faith in God?

What truths or insights deepened your understanding of the character of God?

What presented the greatest challenge in your daily life?

Discovering the Promise

Read Joshua 1:8 in your Bible. Copy it here.

Read Joshua 1:7. What additional direction does God give for ensuring success?

Understanding the Promise

Read 2 Timothy 2:15 and write down God's desire for your Bible study habits.

Read the verses below and note what they say about desiring God and His Word.

Job 23:12—

Psalm 119:103—

Jeremiah 15:16—

Read the verses below, and note what they teach about memorizing Scripture.

Psalm 37:31—

Psalm 40:8—

Psalm 119:11—

Applying the Promise

Which suggestions, activities, or questions regarding success do you think would make the greatest difference in your life, and why?

What can you do to make your answer(s) a reality?

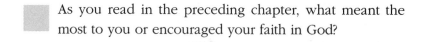

LESSON 22

As you read in the preceding chapter, what meant the most to you or encouraged your faith in God?

What truths or insights deepened your understanding of the character of God?

What presented the greatest challenge in your daily life?

Discovering the Promise

Read 1 Corinthians 15:57 in your Bible. Copy it here.

What are we to give to God, and what does God give to us?

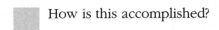 How is this accomplished?

Understanding the Promise

Read 1 Corinthians 15:54, and write out its victory cry.

Read Romans 5:17 and 2 Corinthians 5:21 and note how this victory was secured.

Read Romans 8:37-39. How far-reaching is our victory in Christ?

Read the verses below, and note what they teach regarding death for a believer in Christ.

2 Corinthians 5:6-8—

Philippians 1:21 and 23—

Applying the Promise

Which suggestions, activities, or questions regarding victory do you think would make the greatest difference in your life, and why?

What can you do to make your answer(s) a reality?

LESSON 23

As you read in the preceding chapter, what meant the most to you or encouraged your faith in God?

What truths or insights deepened your understanding of the character of God?

What presented the greatest challenge in your daily life?

Discovering the Promise

Read James 1:5 in your Bible. Copy it here.

Who can—and should—ask God for wisdom?

How is God described?

What is God's powerful promise?

How did King Solomon live out this instruction and promise (1 Kings 3:9-12)?

Understanding the Promise

Read the verses below, and note what they teach about acquiring wisdom.

Proverbs 1:7 and 9:10—

Proverbs 2:4-6—

Read the following verses and note what they teach about seeking wisdom from others.

Proverbs 11:14; 15:22; and 24:6—

Titus 2:3-5—

Applying the Promise

Which suggestions, activities, or questions regarding wisdom do you think would make the greatest difference in your life, and why?

What can you do to make your answer(s) a reality?

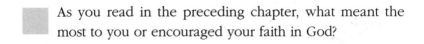

LESSON 24

As you read in the preceding chapter, what meant the most to you or encouraged your faith in God?

What truths or insights deepened your understanding of the character of God?

What presented the greatest challenge in your daily life?

Discovering the Promise

Read Matthew 10:29-31 in your Bible. Copy it here.

List the statements made regarding the following:

sparrows—

the hairs on your head—

the fact of your worth—

Read John 3:16. Exactly how valuable are you according to this verse?

Understanding the Promise

Read the verses below and note the truths they teach about your worth.

Genesis 1:27—

Psalm 139:14—

Romans 5:8—

Applying the Promise

Which suggestions, activities, or questions regarding worth do you think would make the greatest difference in your life, and why?

What can you do to make your answer(s) a reality?

LESSON ABOUT

God's Powerful Promises and Your Character

As you read about character, what meant the most to you or encouraged you to be a man or woman of character?

What truths or insights deepened your understanding of the character of God?

What presented the greatest challenge in your daily life?

Wrapping It Up

As you end your time of considering some of God's powerful promises for you, let's begin to wrap things up and pinpoint some take-away truths. Read the following scriptures and note what they teach about character and character development.

2 Peter 1:5-8—

Galatians 5:22-23—

Which of these character qualities would you like to work on?

A Word of Challenge

Read the following scriptures and note what they teach about character and character development.

Galatians 5:16—

Ephesians 4:1—

Ephesians 5:1-2—

Ephesians 5:3-4—

Colossians 3:8—

Colossians 3:12-14—

Which of these character qualities would you like to work on?

An Opportunity for Application

Putting God's Power to Work

Character counts in all of your relationships and dealings with people. What do you notice about the character—both good and bad—of each of the following husbands and wives?

Ananias and Sapphira—Acts 5:1-4

Zacharias and Elizabeth—Luke 1:5-6

Nabal and Abigail—1 Samuel 25:3

Lot and his wife—Genesis 19:15-17 and 26

One lesson from these couples whether you are married or not is loud and clear: your character or lack of it affects you, your family members, and others!

Notes

1. M.R. DeHaan and Henry G. Bosch, *Our Daily Bread* (Grand Rapids, MI: Zondervan Publishing House, 1982), December 27.

2. Herbert Lockyer, *All the Promises of the Bible* (Grand Rapids, MI: Zondervan Publishing House, 1962), p. 10.

3. Leonard Ravenhill, British evangelist, 1907–1994.

4. Herbert Lockyer, *Daily Promises—Inspiring Devotions for Every Day of the Year* (Peabody, MA: Hendrickson Publishers, Inc., 1996), January 31.

5. Matthew Henry, *Commentary on the Whole Bible* (Peabody, MA: Hendrickson Publishers, Inc., 2003), p. 2280.

6. Alice Gray, *Lists to Live By: The Fourth Collection* (Sisters, OR: Multnomah Publishers, Inc., 2002), pp. 182-83.

7. Michael Kendrick and Daryl Lucas, *365 Life Lessons from Bible People* (Wheaton, IL: Tyndale House Publishers, Inc., 1996), reading #69.

8. H.W. Crocker III, *Robert E. Lee on Leadership—Executive Lessons in Character, Courage, and Vision* (Roseville, CA: Prima Publishing, 2000), p. 35.

9. M.R. DeHaan and Henry G. Bosch, *Bread for Each Day* (Grand Rapids, MI: Zondervan Publishing House, 1980), March 30.

10. Albert M. Wells, Jr., *Inspiring Quotations—Contemporary & Classical*, quoting Bruce Wideman (Nashville, TN: Thomas Nelson Publishers, 1988), p. 199.

11. Matthew Henry, *Commentary on the Whole Bible* (Peabody, MA: Hendrickson Publishers, Inc., 2003), p. 891.

12. John Newton, "Amazing Grace."

13. William MacDonald, *Enjoying the Proverbs*, notes on Proverbs 28:26 (Kansas City, KS: Walterick Publishers, 1982), p. 151.

14. Warren W. Wiersbe, *Be Skillful* (Colorado Springs, CO: Chariot Victor Publishing, 1995), p. 38.

15. Edward Mote, "The Solid Rock."

16. Eleanor Doan, *Speakers Sourcebook* (Grand Rapids, MI: Zondervan Publishing House, 1988), pp. 96, 147.

17. Robert Heinlein, *Stranger in a Strange Land* (additional information unknown).

18. Jim and Elizabeth George, *God Loves His Precious Children*, and Elizabeth George, *Powerful Promises for Every Woman* (Eugene, OR: Harvest House Publishers, 2004 and 2000, respectively).

19. A.J. Gordon (source unknown).

20. Aquila and Priscilla are mentioned in Acts 18:1-3,18-19,26; Romans 16:3-5; 1 Corinthians 16:19.

21. H. Kaveribai, with the last two lines adapted, as quoted in A. Naismith, *A Treasury of Notes, Quotes and Anecdotes* (Grand Rapids, MI: Baker Book House, 1976), p. 167.

22. Author unknown.

23. M.R. DeHaan and Henry G. Bosch, *Our Daily Bread*, September 12.

24. Rick Warren, *The Purpose Driven Life* (Grand Rapids, MI: Zondervan, 2002), p. 17.

25. Francis A. Schaeffer, *Death in the City* (Carol Stream, IL: InterVarsity Press, 1969), chapter 1.

26. Walter B. Knight, *Knight's Treasury of Illustrations*, quoting Tom Roberts in *Moody Monthly* (Grand Rapids, MI: Wm. B. Eerdmans Publishing Company, 1978), p. 310.

27. Jay Kessler, *Parents and Teenagers,* quoting Dwight Spotts, "What Is Child Abuse?" (Wheaton, IL: Victor Books, 1984), p. 426.

28. Benjamin R. DeJong, *Uncle Ben's Quote Book* (Grand Rapids, MI: Baker Book House, 1977), p. 131.

29. J. Oswald Sanders, *Spiritual Leadership* (Chicago: Moody Press, 1976), p. 45.

30. W.E. Vine, *Vine's Expository Dictionary of Old and New Testament Words* (Nashville, TN: Thomas Nelson Publishers, 1997), p. 308.

31. Jim George, *God's Man of Influence* (Eugene, OR: Harvest House Publishers, 2003), p. 84.

32. D.L. Moody as cited in *Northfield Echoes,* vol. 2, ed. D.L. Pierson (East Northfield, MA: Rastall & McKinley, 1895), p. 46.

33. Walter B. Knight, *Knight's Treasury of Illustrations*, no author name given (Grand Rapids, MI: Wm. B. Eerdman's Publishing Company, 1978), p. 422.

34. Saint Bernard of Clairvaux.

35. A.W. Tozer, *The Divine Conquest* (Uhrichsville, OH: Barbour and Company, 1978), chapter 6.

36. Robert Jamieson, A.R. Fausset, and David Brown, *Commentary on the Whole Bible* (Grand Rapids, MI: Zondervan Publishing House, 1971), p. 1254.

Personal Notes

Other Books by Jim George

A Man After God's Own Heart
Many Christian men want to be men after God's own heart...but how do they do this? Jim George shows that a heartfelt desire to practice God's priorities is all that's needed. God's grace does the rest.

A Husband After God's Own Heart
In this Gold-Medallion finalist book, husbands will find their marriages growing richer and deeper as they pursue 12 areas in which they can make a real difference in their relationship with their wives.

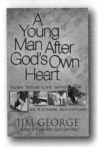

A Young Man After God's Own Heart
Pursuing God really *is* an adventure—a lot like climbing a mountain. There are all kinds of challenges on the way up, but the awesome view at the top is well worth the trip. This book helps young men to experience the thrill of knowing real success in life—the kind that counts with God.

God's Man of Influence
How can a man have a lasting impact? Here are the secrets to having a positive and meaningful influence in the lives of everyone a man meets. This book will help men define the goals that give their lives direction and purpose.

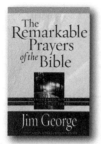

The Remarkable Prayers of the Bible

Jim looks deeply into the prayers of great men and women in the Bible and shares more than a hundred practical applications that can help shape our own lives and prayers. A separate *Growth and Study Guide* is also available.

God Loves His Precious Children

(coauthored with Elizabeth George) Jim and Elizabeth George share the comfort and assurance of Psalm 23 with young children. Engaging watercolor scenes and delightful rhymes bring the truths of each verse to life.

God's Wisdom for Little Boys

(coauthored with Elizabeth George) The wonderful teachings of Proverbs come to life for boys. Memorable rhymes play alongside colorful paintings for an exciting presentation of truths to live by.

An Invitation to Write

Jim George is a teacher and speaker and the author of many books, including *A Man After God's Own Heart*. If you would like to receive more information about other books and audio products by Jim George, to sign up for his mailings, or to share how *What God Wants to Do for You* has influenced your life, you can write to Jim at:

Jim George
P.O. Box 2879
Belfair, WA 98528
Toll-free fax/phone: 1-800-542-4611
www.JimGeorge.com